the australia & new zealand gap pack

Edited by R L Jordan

This second edition published in 2002 in Great Britain by
Gapwork Ltd

  60 Green Road
Meanwood
Leeds
LS6 4JP

  www.gapwork.com
info@gapwork.com

First edition published in 2001

ISBN: 0095404 33 40

Photographs and maps of Australia supplied by kind permission of the
Australian Tourist Commission.

Photographs and map of New Zealand supplied by kind permission of
Tourism New Zealand.

City maps of New Zealand supplied by kind permission of Insight Guides.

Cover design by Anthony Barker at Odd One Out Design.
Content layout design by Gill Varley (www.gillvarley.co.uk).
Printed and bound in Great Britain by Viking Press.

read this first!

★ As you will have noticed we cover Australia and New Zealand. This isn't because the countries are particularly similar (they're not) or because they happen to be our favourite destinations (they are!) It is because as a traveller they are likely to be that rare thing – a long haul destination where you can legally find a job. Even if you are only getting a working holiday visa (WHV) for Australia, the likelihood is you will be travelling to New Zealand at some point. If this is the case, you will find the general information about New Zealand of use, and vice versa if you are planning on working in New Zealand and travelling in Oz. There's nothing stopping you getting a working holiday visa for both countries!

★ The first section of the Pack is what we call our "hosted" section. This is an opportunity for you to get an insight into how specialist companies can turn your working holiday into the trip of a lifetime. Whether it's information on insurance, booking accommodation or sorting your visa, the host companies in this section are the experts.

★ The second section of the Pack is the Gapwork introduction to the real nitty gritty of planning a working holiday downunder. This bit covers taxation, banking and general work information.

★ Thirdly there are the city destination sections, Sydney, Melbourne, Brisbane and Perth.

★ At the end of the Australia section is the Australia Backpacker Web Directory.

★ The New Zealand section begins with more relevant info from hosts. It then follows the same structure as Australia, with general living, travelling and working info followed by the city destinations and the New Zealand Backpacker Web Directory.

★ Finally there is the Gapwork gap year diary. With a page for each week you are away, use the space to make notes about your time travelling. Use our guidelines to help you keep track of the amazing things you do while you are abroad, and how these experiences can improve your skills profile for your CV and job applications.

The Australia & New Zealand Gap Pack has been designed to help you make the most of your time out travelling. Good luck!

contents

Welcome to the Australia and New Zealand Gap Pack!

Gapwork has created the Pack with the unique needs of the working holidaymaker in mind. All of the Gapwork staff are experienced travellers and backpackers. Our own research has shown us what is important to independent travellers, and we have added the expertise of established companies.

Basically there are three things you need as someone planning a long trip overseas: information, information and, erm, information. You then need some common sense and good instinct to sort the wheat from the chaff. Gapwork helps you by having done all the hard graft for you. We have searched the web, sent scouts down under, and contacted hundreds of companies in Australia and New Zealand in order to compile the Pack.

We have focused on Brisbane, Melbourne, Perth and Sydney in Australia, as they are the most popular destinations for working holidaymakers. These are the cities where you will make (and spend) those Aussie dollars. Auckland, Christchurch and Wellington are all cities in New Zealand large enough to take on a travelling workforce.

The host companies featured in the Pack have been assisting travellers for years. Whether it is advice about getting your visa, the best ways to explore Oz and New Zealand or the right agency to get you working, we guarantee that someone in this Pack will be able to help you out.

It's the same issues that come up again and again when people talk to us about getting a job overseas - how to work legally, how to find employers who take on travellers, where to stay, and how much they can expect to earn. Above all, travellers want to know that they will be able to find work, and earn money. The last thing they want is to have to return home early because they have run out of cash. Gapwork has come up with the Gap Pack as an answer to these questions and more.

So for the time being, let us do the hard work and you just lie back and think of Australia....

www.fco.gov.uk/knowbeforeyougo
for essential travel advice and tips

The British Foreign & Commonwealth Office has launched a campaign promoting safe travel. Go to...

www.fco.gov.uk/knowbeforeyougo
to check safety reports on countries, find out more about your destination and browse through their backpacker section.

visas

Working holiday visas

TRAVELLERS
CONTACT POINT
AUSTRALIA • NEW ZEALAND • UNITED KINGDOM

To work in Australia you need to apply for a Working Holiday Visa (Form 1150). This cannot be granted in Australia but certain nationalities (including British people) may apply in any country except Australia.

Citizens of the following countries can obtain a Working Holiday Visa (WHV) for Australia in the UK: Canada, Denmark, Finland, Ireland, the Netherlands, Sweden, Norway and the UK.

You have a year from the date your visa is issued in which to travel to Australia and you are allowed to stay in Australia for 12 months from the date you enter. You can travel in and out of Australia as many times as you like during the 12 months from the date of first entry. However if you depart Australia during your 12 months stay you can't "top up" or recover the period of time spent outside Australia. You are only ever issued one WHV.

The work restrictions on the visa mean you can only work for three months with any one employer, however there are no restrictions on the type of work you can do. A WHV also allows you to study or do training in Australia for up to three months as part of your year there.

A Working Holiday Visa is the best way of working legally and getting paid properly on your travels. If you are doing a round the world trip, Australia and New Zealand will be your likely port of calls for holiday and work. There are a number of criteria you must fulfil as a working holiday visa applicant for Australia:

★ You must be aged between 18 and 30 at the time you make your application.

★ Have no dependent children.

★ You must have enough money in your bank account (AUD$5,000, about £2,000) when you apply to show that you will be able to support yourself in Australia.

★ The main purpose of your visit to Australia should be for a holiday, not to work.

★ Meet health and character requirements.

★ Upon arrival be able to provide an outward ticket or sufficient funds for one.

If you need a Form 1150 please call Travellers Contact Point and they will send you one plus a complete working holiday kit for free. They provide a visa processing service for only £15 plus the embassy fee (currently £70).

australia

Other types of visas

ETA (Electronic Travel Authority)

All travellers to Australia (other than NZ citizens) require a visa. An ETA is issued electronically and is valid for 12 months allowing you to stay up to 3 months at a time in Australia. You can get an ETA from the Australian Embassy by applying online (for a charge of $20) and travel agents (the cost will vary from £10 - £14). Travellers Contact Point provide a quick and easy service for only £10, just call with your passport details.

It is strictly against the law to work on a visitor visa in Australia. Illegal labour is a political hot topic in Australia and the Department of Immigration will be only too happy to add you to the statistics of illegal workers they have caught and deported!

Tourist visitor visas

This visa does not allow you to work but you can visit Australia for up to six months. You are required to show that you are able to support yourself financially and it is open to any age group. The embassy charge is currently £30, if you would like some assistance with your application Travellers Contact Point provide a processing service for only £15.

Student visas

The Australian government operates an Overseas Student Program (OSP) that allows people who are not Australian citizens to study in Australia. You must obtain a student visa (Form 157A) before you can commence a course of study in Australia. You can be granted a student visa only if you wish to undertake a registered course or part of a registered course on a full-time basis. Students on this scheme can work up to 20 hours per week and up to 40 hours during school holidays (around 12 weeks school holidays per year). Travellers Contact Point represent several approved colleges and universities in and around Sydney.

The Student Visa scheme is a great alternative to the working holiday for those of you torn between taking a "gap year" and continuing with your studies. It is also suitable for those of you who have already used the once in a lifetime Working Holiday Visa to return for another extended stay, and a good opportunity if you're looking to migrate. Studying in Australia and getting a qualification there can boost your migration points by up to 65 (110 is required to be eligible to apply for migration).

Other visas such as those enabling permanent immigration, temporary employment or business in Australia are much harder to get than the tourist or working holiday visa. Getting one involves a lot of paperwork, time and effort with potential employers and lawyers. If you are eligible, a working holiday visa is by far the easiest way to work legally in Australia whilst travelling.

Travellers Contact Point:

info@travellersuk.com

020 7243 7887

Image courtesy of Australian Tourist Commission

hosts

more info

sydney

melbourne

brisbane

perth

web

10. australia & new zealand gap pack

Accommodation

One of the first things to worry travellers is finding somewhere to stay. Most travellers heading to Oz will make a beeline for a hostel (or "backpackers" as the Aussies imaginatively call them). But how can you find a hostel that is right for you?

Ask yourself the following questions...

☑ How much can I spend? Prices will vary according to the season, the individual hostel, and the type of room you want.

☑ Where do I want to be? Do you want to stay in a city centre near bars and clubs? Or would you rather head for the quieter suburbs?

☑ How long do I want to stay there? If you are planning on spending a long time in one place, you will need to look for short term rented accommodation payable by the month, rather than the night.

☑ Could I work there? If you are thinking of staying for a shorter time, but still long enough to see the bills mount up, you could negotiate a deal whereby you work in the hostel and get free accommodation.

☑ What kind of room do I want? If you are travelling alone or in a group, a dormitory will definitely be the cheapest option. If you are a couple and need some privacy, you'll have to stump up more for a room.

☑ What kind of hostel do I want? Some hostels are run by chains and have hundreds of beds with lots of facilities - bar, off license, job centre, swimming pool etc. These tend to be in city centres and can be a bit impersonal if you are looking to make friends with fellow travellers or Australians. At the other end of the scale are small outfits that are often run by ex-travellers. In between comes everything else, but in the aftermath of the hostel fire in Queensland in 2000, safety is an issue. To be on the safe side, when you first arrive and need to get your bearings, prepare to pay a little more for a central hostel with a good reputation.

Many hostels will have facilities for luggage storage, but you may have to resign yourself to the fact that you will have to leave your rucksack unattended in the dormitories at certain times. Just make sure that you carry all your important stuff, documents, money and things of personal value with you.

Going abroad this year?

Think you've remembered everything?

Have you checked the FCO country travel advice, and taken out adequate insurance cover?

- **Never travel without adequate insurance cover (even on short breaks).**
  Check policy exemptions carefully, and make sure you declare any pre-existing medical conditions to your insurer.

- **Check out your destination.**
  FCO country travel advice is available on the Internet at **www.fco.gov.uk** *or by calling* **020 7008 0232/0233.**

- **Travelling within the European Union?**
  Get Form E111 from the Post Office for reduced or free emergency care. But you should still take out adequate insurance cover.

- **Avoid any involvement with drugs.**
  The penalties are severe and could include the death sentence.

- **British consular officers are ready to help you if you get into difficulties abroad.**
  Make a note of the telephone number of the nearest British Consulate.

Foreign & Commonwealth Office Travel Advice:

Internet: **www.fco.gov.uk**

Tel: **020 7008 0232/0233** *Fax:* **020 7008 0155** www.fco.gov.uk/knowbeforeyougo

accommodation

You can read up details on all the hostels before you head-off at

 www.hostelworld.com

Hostelworld also feature hostel reviews from other travellers on items such as character, location, fun, security and staff. These are independent reviews from people who have stayed in this hostel before so should give you a good indication of the standard.

For those of you landing in to Sydney or Melbourne on a longer stay think about booking a Starter Pack – many hostels offer these and you can read all about them on Hostelworld.com. Starter Packs generally include your first few night's accommodation, an airport transfer and a free tour of the city. Many also add in help and advice on getting your tax file number and assistance with getting a job or a flat.

Don't forget that Hostelworld.com also offer information and online bookings for all your tours and activities in Australia. So before you dive the reef, bus it up the East Coast or bungee-jump off a bridge, check out the best deals at Hostelworld.com.

Some useful accommodation websites:

 www.hostelworld.com - Book hostels and get info online

 www.hostelaustralia.com

Image courtesy of Australian Tourist Commission

hosts

more info

sydney

melbourne

brisbane

perth

web

Insurance

Getting the proper insurance is important for your trip. A good gap year policy will be tailored to the particular needs of backpackers. Your luggage as a

backpacker is probably only going to consist of a rucksack with a few clothes, so most policies don't insure your luggage for a huge amount.

The medical cover you receive is very important as you may be travelling in developing countries where the medical services are not up to western standards. Even in developed countries, health services work differently and you may have to pay more for certain things. Medical treatment is very expensive wherever you are, and if something really drastic happened to you whilst you were abroad, the costs could be astronomical. Most gap year insurance packages cover repatriation costs, meaning that they would pay for you to be flown home if you were seriously ill. Some will cover the cost of having a family member flown out to you in an emergency. Knowing you are covered for most eventualities gives you the peace of mind to really enjoy your gap year.

Insurance checklist...

☑ How long am I insured for?
☑ Where in the world will the insurance policy cover me?
☑ What happens if I lose or have my passport stolen?
☑ What happens if someone steals my wallet?
☑ Am I covered for extreme sports and adventure activities?
☑ What happens if I need to go hospital?
☑ What happens if I miss my flight?
☑ What happens if I have to do exam retakes?
☑ Will I get flown home if I need to?

☺ **Tip:**

Take the contact phone number of your insurance company with you in case of emergency. Carry it around with you in your money belt, in your rucksack and in your wallet. Also copy the policy number and any other reference you will need if you have to contact them. Photocopy the insurance documents and take them with you on your travels. Read the small print of the policy – many policies don't cover you if you have an accident whilst on a motorbike, and don't cover your property if it is left in a car overnight (unless it is locked in the boot).

 www.navigatortravel.co.uk

Side tabs: hosts | more info | sydney | melbourne | brisbane | perth | web

australia

Tours

The Backpackers Travel Centre does it all.
Travel by coach, plane and foot; overnight stays in hostels, camping villages and dorms; the nitty gritty and necessary things that have to be done before you embark upon the trip of a lifetime! So who better to talk to than experienced backpackers themselves, which is what the BTC staff are.

Coach travel is a cheap and fun way to travel, especially when taking an organised tour. When one country is as big as the whole of Europe, and New Zealand is almost the size of the UK alone, you need some professional help to make sure you make the most of your visit!

Backpackers Travel Centre (BTC) works closely with over 100 different backpacker tour operators and adventure groups in Australia – that means that they work with every type of company you could need when travelling to Australia, from accommodation and tours when you arrive in Australia, through to travel insurance and visas.

There are literally dozens upon dozens of things to see in Australia so you'll want to make the most of your time over there. The BTC Travel Crew can help you plan an itinerary for all or part of your trip, depending on how long you're going for, making sure that you cover all of the famed sites in your plans.

BTC can also arrange your flight to Australia, with a stop over in Singapore, Thailand or Bangkok for example, if you fancy seeing another country before you arrive in Oz. They use a variety of airlines so can arrange for a quote for you – all you need to do is ask.

A typical itinerary might include Ayers Rock, Alice Springs, the Blue Mountains, Surfers Paradise, the Great Ocean Road, and Fraser Island – that's not including any of the sights and experiences of Sydney, Melbourne and Perth!

Backpackers Travel Centre has 26 offices in key destinations around Australia and New Zealand to help you when you arrive. They now have two in the UK to help you get started before you leave, so you can start planning the basics. BTC want to ensure that you have all of your questions answered and your dream trip planned perfectly.

tours

hosts

more info

sydney

melbourne

brisbane

perth

web

A great way to get an idea of all of the places in Australia that you might want to visit is to have a look through brochures. BTC have produced a fantastic 70 page glossy brochure "Backpacking Australia". This summarises what each of BTC's main suppliers can offer you, how much the tours cost, along with when and where you can take the tours.

To request a free copy of this brochure, please email...

     london@backpackerstravel.net.au

or call free on

☎   0800 376 1045.

BTC's London offices are in Earls Court and Fulham Broadway, so feel free to go along and see them if you'd like any more information or simply want to pick their brains!

🕸   www.backpackerstravel.org

Image courtesy of Australian Tourist Commission

Driving

To drive in Australia you will need a full driving licence. You will need to carry your licence with you at all times – there is an on the spot fine for not doing so. Australians drive on the left hand side of the road, and the speed limits are 35mph/60kmph in built up areas and 60mph/100kmph on country roads and highways.

It is compulsory to wear seatbelts front and back at all times, and the laws on drink driving are enforced very strictly. Random breath testing is common as are speed traps.

Petrol or diesel costs between 80 cents and 1 dollar per litre. You can check prices (if you are that bothered!) at

 www.informedsources.com.au/petrol/default.htm

If you are planning on going off the beaten track then be sure that you have a full tank of fuel. Rural garages tend to shut earlier and may not take credit card payments.

Driving is one of the best ways to see Australia, and can be an unforgettable experience. Use your common sense when heading inland and into bush areas. Make sure you have plenty of supplies, including fuel, water and food. Also leave your travel itinerary with a friend – make sure someone knows where you are planning on going and when you will get to your destination.

Many hire firms operate a one-way hire service, so you can hire from Cairns and drop off in Sydney. The minimum rental age is 21. One or two companies also offer a Buyback Guarantee on cars for sale, which means you are guaranteed a fixed amount when you sell your car back at the end of your trip. But beware of dodgy operators: try to ask other travellers about their experiences with particular firms. You can do this online by going to the Thorn Tree message boards at

 www.lonelyplanet.com

Hitching lifts is not recommended in any country. You are potentially leaving yourself open to all kinds of dangers, and who wants to be stuck in a lorry cab with a stranger for days in the middle of nowhere?

If you are buying a vehicle when you arrive in Oz you will need to check the state registration requirements. There are official websites where you can check vehicle registration requirements, road laws and advice on driving in our Australia Backpacker Web Directory at the back of this section.

hosts

more info

sydney

melbourne

brisbane

perth

web

Image courtesy of Australian Tourist Commission

Driver fatigue is responsible for almost one fifth of fatal crashes in Australia. You should allow time for fifteen minute breaks every two hours on your journey. When you are driving long distances through countryside beware of the animals that often stray onto the road. Road kill is a common sight on the freeway, and we're talking six-foot kangaroos jumping out in front of your van....

 www.travellers-autobarn.com

Reasons to drive yourself in Oz

★ If a group of 2 or 3 or more band together and share costs then it actually the cheapest form of travel possible.
★ You can snog in the back of the car.
★ You can pull over and camp for free in many places.
★ You don't have to pay extra for side trips, you can simply drive yourself.
★ You can play your own tunes.
★ You can stop if you see something interesting.

Image courtesy of Australian Tourist Commission

hosts

more info

sydney

melbourne

brisbane

perth

web

organised schemes

australia

A working holiday in
Australia
made easy with **BUNAC!**

Taking part in BUNAC's *Work Australia* programme offers the exciting prospect of working and travelling for up to a year on the other side of the planet. Likely to appeal to gap years, recent graduates or those looking to take time out from their career, the programme allows you to spend extended time in another culture and work to finance your travels. Visiting places like Sydney Harbour, Ayers Rock, Perth and the Great Barrier Reef is all part of the experience.

Programme benefits include:

♦ Round-the-world flight ticket valid for a full 18 months

♦ Working holiday visa – we obtain the visa for you

♦ Organised two-day stopover in either Hong Kong or Bangkok

♦ Group flights – meet fellow travellers before you get there

♦ Support services of BUNAC's subsidiary in Sydney – for help and advice on finding work and accommodation, travel tips and much much more.

Programme open to students and non-students aged 18-30.
Flights normally run from July to March.

For more information on BUNAC's *Work Australia* programme or to download the Application Form, log onto www.bunac.org

Dept. GP1, BUNAC, 16 Bowling Green Lane,
London EC1R 0QH   E-mail: enquiries@bunac.org.uk

Tel: 020 7251 3472

WWW.BUNAC.ORG

organised schemes

Organised schemes

Arriving in Australia without any definite plans can be quite daunting especially when it is so far away from home and such a huge country. If you are a bit wary of going it alone, you may prefer to enrol on an organised working holiday in Oz. There are various organisations which provide such schemes and one of the best known ones is BUNAC's Work Australia programme.

BUNAC is a non-profit organisation which arranges work and travel programmes for students and young people to various countries. The Work Australia programme allows participants to take any job, anywhere in Australia. The programme goes beyond the existing Australian Government Working Holidaymaker scheme by providing BUNAC's back-up help and support both before departure and throughout your stay through BUNAC's subsidiary IEP. IEP takes care of you on arrival, providing support, accommodation during arrival and orientation, as well as job and travel hints and 'on-the-spot' assistance when needed. The group flight departures also provide the ideal opportunity to meet with fellow participants.

 www.bunac.org

Case study

Emma Yates spent her gap year as a participant on BUNAC's Work Australia programme.

"I set off on BUNAC's Work Australia programme with visions of a world of sun and surf. Australia was certainly this but also a whole lot more. The diversity and sheer vastness of this country is nothing less than incredible. My adventure began with 40 other BUNACers, eight of whom were to be my flatmates in Sydney for the following three months. After a few days, nine of us moved into a luxury apartment near Darling Harbour and by then I'd also found work as a waitress at the harbour. I spent the next nine months travelling through every state and territory, working to earn money as I went along.

Some of my favourite memories are doing voluntary work out in the Australian bush of the Northern Territories in a place called Rum Jungle. I'd never pictured myself shovelling manure on an organic farm in the blistering heat but watching the most amazing sunsets from our roof at the end of the day with a glass of ice cold beer in hand more than made up for it! My other good memories were spotting my first kangaroo, going to an Aussie Rules football game, learning to surf and sleeping out in 'swags' under the stars even though we did get rained on! In fact no two days on the road were ever the same. From the exciting cities of Sydney and Melbourne, the rainforests and mountains of Tasmania and the deep red soil of the Australian outback – this is a country where you can find it all."

tax

Tax File Number

Everyone who wants to work in Australia needs a Tax File Number. You will need your passport and your working holiday visa to collect it from any of the offices listed below. You should get your tax file number sorted as soon as you arrive in Australia as it can take up to three weeks to arrive.

★ Sydney Tax Office - 100 Market Street
★ Brisbane Tax Office - 280 Adelaide Street
★ Melbourne Tax Office - Casseldon Place, 2 Lonsdale Street
★ Perth Tax Office - 45 Francis Street, Northbridge

The central phone number for tax office enquiries and appointments is 13 2861. For refund and tax file number enquiries call 13 2863. (Phone numbers beginning "13" with no area code are central phone numbers for a large organization)

Tax Refunds

The basic rate of tax you will pay, as a working holidaymaker is 29%. If you have worked for a while and believe you are entitled to some tax back, ESS can help you reclaim your tax by doing the refund application for you. Contact Australia@ess.ie to guarantee your maximum tax refund, in the quickest time possible. ESS Tax Refunds will give you a free quote on how much tax you are due back.

★ The average refund from Australia is £720.00 sterling.
★ You may work during two tax years, in which case you would be due two tax refunds from Australia.
★ ESS can even forward your refund to you in Australia as you continue your travels!

☺ **Tip:**

The number of employers you have will affect your refund amount. Contact Australia@ess.ie for more information.

Register online: www.ess.ie/gapwork
To ensure a rapid tax refund, forward your Group certificates/final pay slips to:

✉ ESS Tax Refunds, 20 Eden Quay, Dublin 1, Ireland
☎ +353 1 670 6959, fax: +353 1 878 3350
✆ info@ess.ie   www.ess.ie

You will need to give a written request to your employer, at least 14 days in advance of leaving, for your Group Certificate. If you lose your Group Certificates/Final Payment slips from your employer, don't worry as ESS can apply for replacements. ESS can organise your tax refunds if you have worked in Australia, Japan, the UK, Germany, New Zealand, Holland, Ireland, Canada and the USA.

getting there

Flights

Buying your flight to Australia should be easy. Do so by calling into a high street travel agent, or by using the Internet. Research prices online and in the adverts in the travel sections of newspapers before paying for a flight.

How much you pay depends on when you fly. The busiest times for flights are around school holidays in July, August and December, and this is when flights will be more expensive. The Australian spring begins in September, and the summer ends in February, so this part of the year is also popular in terms of visitor arrivals. Travelling at Christmas can mean booking flights months in advance, and paying more. If you were to wait until January, the price of flights will drop. Sydney is the most popular city to fly into.

Australia is a long way from the UK – a flight can take up to 25 hours, depending on your route. Stopovers in Bangkok or Singapore are the most popular option for backpackers.

Jetlag

One of the main problems with long haul flights is that crossing time zones disrupts your sleep patterns and causes jet lag. Travelling eastwards is more likely to make you jetlagged than going west. Symptoms include tiredness, irritability, forgetfulness and disorientation. This can be a real problem if as well as arriving in a strange country; you have to cope with feeling jet lagged. You can help prevent jet lag by getting a good night's sleep the night before you travel, drinking plenty of water, stretching regularly during the flight and taking daytime flights.

To give yourself time to adapt to new time zones and recover from jet lag, allow one day's recovery for every time zone you cross.

Economy class syndrome

Travelling for hours on a plane is not good for your circulation. Economy Class Syndrome is the commonly used name for deep vein thrombosis (DVT). DVT happens when a blood clot forms after being sat in cramped conditions for a long period of time. It is relatively rare, but research on the subject shows that it may be more of a problem than previously thought. The condition can be fatal.

By simply moving around during the flight, walking up and down the aisle, stretching and drinking plenty of water you reduce the chances of contracting DVT. Taking sleeping pills or drinking excessive alcohol during the flight is not recommended. The more mobile and active you are, the better. Smokers, obese people and women who are pregnant or using the contraceptive pill are at more risk of developing DVT.

getting around

hosts

more info

sydney

melbourne

brisbane

perth

web

Public transport

The alternative to organised tours designed for backpackers is using public transport. The downside to public transport is that the routes are the quickest way of getting from a to b, rather than going to places of specific interest to travellers. And of course you don't have tour guides or pre-organised accommodation.

Greyhound buses

"The country's only national coach company" according to their website. Their Aussie Explorer passes are available at a discount with a recognised student/backpacker membership card (i.e. YHA, VIP or Nomads).

McCafferty's Express Coaches

With 3,6 and 12-month Travel Australia Passes you save up to 50% off normal fares. "Australia's oldest and most successful private coach service." (Recently merged with Greyhound).

Rail travel and flights are the other most popular ways of getting around Australia. The Indian Pacific train journey from Sydney to Perth, and the Ghan route from Melbourne to Alice Springs are both world famous train journeys, taking in amazing scenery.

Recent developments in the internal flights market mean prices are very reasonable. However it may be cheaper to book internal flights in advance with your travel agent before you arrive in Australia. See our Australia Backpacker Web Directory for listings of airlines and rail companies.

Image courtesy of Australian Tourist Commission

what to take

Get your kit off...

One of the most common questions asked by people thinking of going backpacking is – "what do I need to take?"

Buying a rucksack

Your first concern should be a rucksack. Two things are important when choosing your rucksack: the first is fit, and the second is capacity.

The fit of the rucksack is vital because you are very likely to be carrying it for a lot of the time. Wandering round a hot city trying to find a hostel with a 60-litre pack straining at your shoulders is not a good way of starting your holiday.

Always buy a rucksack after you have tried it on (with weight in it). You are most likely to be buying a rucksack with an internally built frame, as these are good for comfort, flexibility and balance. Frameless rucksacks are more likely to be used for daypacks or climbing and other activities where flexibility is required. Rucksacks with external frames are an older design and are most appropriate for very heavy loads that need to be piled high on the back.

When you are trying on your rucksack, all the weight should be on your hips rather than on your shoulders. You should feel the weight being carried around the small of your back. This is where your natural centre of balance is.

A problem that some internal framed rucksacks have is that the surface that is against your back can prevent air circulation. This means that you'll have a hot, sweaty back – not what you need when trekking through a tropical rainforest! Make sure that any parts of the rucksack that will be in contact with your skin are made of breathable, open cell foam. This should assist air circulation.

Size does matter. Too big and you'll be tempted to pack your entire life into it before you go. Too small and you'll just end up buying a bigger rucksack later on in your travels. For a long journey expect to need a good 60-litre rucksack.

Some manufacturers have designed rucksacks especially for women. These are shorter in the back, slightly narrower and have different hip and belt adjustment straps. Another development is the Travel Pack, a kind of cross between a rucksack and a holdall. It looks like a rucksack, but has a zip down it and adjustable straps so you can carry it like a case if you need to. These tend to be more expensive, and bear in mind that the more zips you have on a rucksack, the more likely it is that water can get in, and zips can break. Travel packs can be a good option if you are not planning on doing a lot of real trekking or hiking, if you are planning on spending long periods in one place, and if you need to arrive somewhere looking smarter than your average backpacker.

When you have found a rucksack which is the right size, the right price and suitable for your journey, do a last check:

- ☑ Are the seams double or triple sewn?
- ☑ Are major seams covered or sealed?
- ☑ Is the rucksack as waterproof as possible?
- ☑ Is it made out of heavy-duty nylon?
- ☑ Is the base of the rucksack thicker than the rest of it?

What should I pack?
Size may matter but less is definitely more when it comes to packing.

☺   Some basic tips:
Pack the heaviest stuff at the bottom and towards the inside of the rucksack (i.e. against your back). Pack the things which you will need most often near the top. Be ruthless. Books are heavy to carry and you can buy them anywhere, likewise toiletries.

f you are planning on going into the Outback or bush, the Police Department of Western Australia recommend that you pack the following:

- ☑ Water bottle (with water in it!).
- ☑ Survival knife (Swiss army multi purpose type).
- ☑ Plastic bags for use as water collectors.
- ☑ Foil rescue blanket for shelter, warmth and as a signalling aid if you get into trouble.
- ☑ Nylon cord for multiple uses.
- ☑ Canvas tape for first aid and repairs.
- ☑ Hand mirror for signalling aid.
- ☑ Waterproof matches.
- ☑ Water purifying tablets.
- ☑ Barley sugar for energy food source.

You should also bring a ground sheet and a sleeping bag liner if you are planning on camping. And a tent, obviously!

hosts

more info

sydney

melbourne

brisbane

perth

web

Office work

 Note:
The average adult weekly wage in Australia is around AUS $860.

 www.abs.gov.au

Working holidays in Oz don't have to mean glass collecting or fruitpicking. If you have office skills then use them! Bear in mind however that on a working holiday visa you can only work for three months with any one employer, so you are unlikely to appeal to many employers who would prefer to have long term staff. For this reason temping agencies are your best bet. In all larger cities there is a well-established supply of, and demand for temporary staff with working holiday visas.

If you're thinking of taking time out to go travelling, you are probably going to have to work whilst you are overseas. Although there are more backpackers in Oz than ever before, and the economy has seen better times, experienced staff will always be required by good agencies.

A copy of your CV can be saved on your email. This means you can simply print it off when you need it, without getting it crumpled up in your backpack. Take a smart outfit for interviews and work, or you can always budget to buy a suit and some shoes when you are over there. Clothes tend to be cheaper in Australia than in the UK or Ireland.

At Christmas and New Year there are considerably less office temp opportunities throughout Australia. Offices close for the holidays and businesses are winding down. A better time of year is around May/June, when the tax year is ending and businesses are doing a lot of bookwork.

Office Admin & Secretarial
Office agencies are looking for people with the full range of secretarial and admin skills. If you know how to use Microsoft applications and have a typing speed of 55wpm or over, then contact an employment agency. You can email your CV to one of the agencies in this Pack, or give them a call when you arrive.

In a secretarial/office support role you can expect to earn between AUS$16 to AUS$25 per hour, depending on your skills and the position.

IT & Accounting
If you are a qualified accountant then you should not need to pick fruit or be a lap dancer on your travels (unless you want to!) Along with accountancy IT is a sector where skilled people are in demand. Experience in programming languages, operating systems, databases and internet technologies are especially sought after.

hosts

more info

sydney

melbourne

brisbane

perth

web

work

Hospitality work

Working in bars, hotels, restaurants and resorts is an obvious way to earn money whilst in Australia. Hotel, tourism and leisure companies need most staff during school holidays, at Easter and Christmas. Resorts have the highest demand for staff in the summer, which is December to February. If you are looking for a solid three months of work, this can be a good opportunity to head to the Gold or Sunshine Coast. Think about the west coast if you are looking for resort work at this time of year. It has many beautiful resorts, and there isn't as much competition for work from other travellers.

Keeping your black and whites at the ready is a sure way to impress catering agencies and restaurants. If you don't have room in your rucksack, budget for a pair of tailored black trousers, a plain white shirt and some black shoes when you get to Australia. Clothes are generally cheaper than in the UK. Black shoes should be plain, preferably lace ups, and should cover the whole of your foot (don't turn up in sandals!)

Aussie bars and restaurants love experienced staff. The more bar and waiting experience you can get before you leave, the better.

If you have worked in an upmarket restaurant before, you stand more chance of getting work in a place with good tips in Oz. Beware though – tipping isn't as common in Australia as it is elsewhere.

"A la carte" experience is something that ads for waiting staff frequently require. It basically means you will be expected to show the customer to their table, hand out menus and take orders from the table. Silver service looks good on your CV too.

If you can make a cappuccino or espresso using a proper coffee machine, you will be able to get a lot more work in cafes and bars.

The RSA (Responsible Serving of Alcohol) certificate is useful if you are planning on doing a lot of bar work. Hospitality agencies will charge you a fee to do your course, which takes around 4 hours to complete. Many bars and restaurants require their staff to have this qualification, particularly in New South Wales.

If you have good references bring them with you to show to employers. It could give you the edge over other applicants having them to hand.

Each state has its own "award rate" or minimum wage for work in the hospitality and catering sector. Check out...

    www.wagenet.gov.au

for up to date information on this. As a rough guide however you can expect to earn per hour:
Waiter - $14 to $21; Chef - $21 to $28; Kitchen hand - $13 to $20.

Nursing

There are two types of nurse in Australia:

★ Registered nurse – university educated and qualified.
★ Enrolled nurse – an enrolled nurse works under the supervision of a registered nurse.

To work as a nurse in Australia with a working holiday visa you should apply to the Nurse Registration Authority (NRA) in the state or territory in which you wish to work. You should do this before you arrive in Australia. Nurses have to be registered in the state they wish to practise in. The NRA will check that you can demonstrate that you meet the national nursing competency standards that are required for all territories.

Some nationalities have to do a "competency based assessment program" when they arrive in Oz. If you are from the UK, Ireland or Canada, you don't have to.

If you are not on a WHV, you will have to go through the Australian Nursing Council (ANCI) to complete an assessment, which costs $500. WHV holders do not have to do this, but ANCI recommend that you do as it can save you time (apparently) when you try to register with the state Nurses Regulatory Authority.

If you have registered with the NRA in Queensland for example, you can work in other states as they have a mutual recognition of registration. This also applies to New Zealand. However, you will still have to pay a separate registration fee for each state or territory you wish to work in.

Your union in your home country should be able to help you find out about work overseas. If you're registering with an Australian employment agency they will be able to help you with documentation and red tape.

hosts

more info

sydney

melbourne

brisbane

perth

web

work

Teaching

The federal system in Australia means that each state and territory has different rules and regulations for registering overseas qualified teachers.

The schools system in Australia has three basic levels:
* ★ pre-school education
* ★ primary education
* ★ secondary education

Pre-school education is not compulsory and ranges from part time to full time, depending on which state you are in.

Children start primary education at 5 or 6 years old, again depending on state legislation. The primary school curriculum includes English, maths, science, history, geography, technology, arts and PE. It is not uncommon for a primary school to teach a second language as well as English. One class teacher teaches most major subjects and stays with the class through the day.

A child's attendance at secondary school is compulsory until they are 15 or 16, depending on state or territory legislation. Secondary school teachers should be able to teach at least two subjects to a high level.

An Australian teacher will have done at least four years full time study. This will include a minimum of six weeks full time supervised teaching practice.

Australian secondary schools are mostly comprehensive high schools. The last two years of secondary education may be taught in specialist colleges. Apart from state schools, there are also many Catholic, charitably funded and independent schools in Australia. In line with the size and variety of the country, the range of schools goes from large urban schools to one-teacher outfits in tiny rural towns.

As someone on a working holiday visa you will be eligible to apply for teaching on a casual status. You will need to obtain a Casual Approved Number from the department of education in the state you want to work in. You will also need a full transcript of all the courses and your university qualifications including your degree and/or diploma certificates. Casual supply teachers are often thrown in at the deep end - you could be working in particularly poor or run down schools where the usual teachers are often on leave. Prepare yourself for this aspect of the work.

Areas where there are particular shortages of teachers include maths, science and languages.

You must register as a teacher before you can begin work. In Queensland and Southern Australia, all teachers must be registered. The Registered Schools Board must register all teachers in non-government schools in Victoria.

In New South Wales and Western Australia your eligibility to teach is determined by the relevant Department of Education for government schools. Non-government schools are able to decide for themselves who they will employ.

If you are on a working holiday visa, you must contact the relevant authority to establish your credentials and make sure your experience matches the state requirements. See city teaching pages of the Pack for contact details of State Educational Departments.

hosts

more info

sydney

melbourne

brisbane

perth

web

work

Harvest work

Australia has a huge farming industry and fruitpicking is a tried and tested form of backpacker graft. It can be hard work, and it won't make you rich, but fruit picking is a good way to see other bits of the country and meet people. One of the reasons that the Australian government is so keen to set up working holiday programmes with other countries is that there is a chronic shortage of workers to do harvesting.

Harvesting can involve a lot of different tasks, everything from fruitpicking to driving the tractors or feeding the workers. You name it – Australia grows it. Apricots, asparagus, melons, bananas - you could pick them all.

 Case study

Mildura is in North Western Victoria and is known as the "gateway to the Outback". Between February and April there is lots of work and they encourage travellers with working holiday visas to come along. You would be picking grapes for drying, and would be paid piecework. Apparently an average picker will get through 200 buckets of sultanas a day, for which you would get around AUS$80. You work a six-day week. Some growers provide huts for pickers to sleep and cook in, but if you have a tent you will be at an advantage as accommodation is limited. You will be working in temperatures of around 20 – 35 degrees, with an early start to avoid the worst of the afternoon sun. Expect to be paid one week after you start.

You will need...

- ☑ To be relatively fit!
- ☑ Comfortable shoes which are safe for standing in fields all day
- ☑ A hat
- ☑ A water bottle
- ☑ Sun block
- ☑ Insect repellent

You should also bring some cash to tide you over in case the weather puts back the harvest.

banks

Bank accounts

Opening a bank account in Australia is necessary if you want to work for agencies or established businesses. You will need a passport and a permanent address. The banks listed here are the larger ones who have the most branches nationwide. The branch listed is just one of the more centrally located in each city.

Sydney

★ ANZ, 275 George Street - 131314
★ Commonwealth, 234 William Street - 13 2221
★ Westpac, 60 Martin Place - 13 2032

Brisbane

★ ANZ, 324 Queen Street - 131314
★ Commonwealth, 240 Queen Street - 07 3237 3067

Melbourne

★ ANZ, 254 Queen Street - 131314
★ Commonwealth, 463 Elizabeth Street - 132221

Perth

★ ANZ, 77 St Georges Terrace - 08 9323 8111
★ Commonwealth, 150 St Georges Terrace - 08 9482 6000
★ Westpac, St Georges Terrace - 13 2032

The points system

Australian Banks require you to fulfil a "points" score for ID purposes before you open an account with them. There is nothing sinister about this. Basically you need 100 points to open an account. Your passport is worth 60 points. A driving licence with photo is worth 40 points. So if you have these then you're sorted! If you don't have a driving licence, then a birth certificate is also worth 40 points, a switch card or visa card is worth 25. However you do it, opening a bank account in Australia is actually easier than opening one in the UK. Do try to get a bank account sorted out in the first few weeks of arriving in Australia. The longer you leave it, the more difficult it is to arrange. EFTPOS is an Australian kind of debit card, it is particularly useful for supermarket shopping and using in cash points. You may be offered one with your Aussie bank account.

Getting a permanent address

You will need a permanent address to get a bank account and tax file number. Permanent addresses are defined differently depending on the bank, but most travellers use either a PO Box, a holding address, a hostel address, or the address of a friend in Australia.

Embassies

Your embassy can help you out in a number of ways if you get into trouble or fall seriously ill whilst you're abroad. They can contact your relatives, issue emergency passports and help you transfer money. If you need a doctor or a lawyer whilst abroad they can find one for you. They can even loan you enough money to get home in desperate circumstances. Hopefully you won't have to call on them!

To reduce the chances of having an accident, falling ill or being the victim of crime whilst you are abroad, check the British Foreign and Commonwealth Office website at:

    www.fco.gov.uk/knowbeforeyougo

The "Know Before You Go" campaign was set up by the Foreign Office in order to reduce the number of travellers going to their overseas consuls with problems that could have been prevented. The aim of the campaign is to raise traveller's awareness of the issues that need to be sorted out before they leave the country.

Image courtesy of Australian Tourist Commission

British Consulate in Sydney
- Level 16, The Gateway, 1 Macquarie Place, Sydney, NSW 2000
- ☎ (02) 9247 7521
- bcgsyd1@uk.emb.gov.au

British Consulate in Brisbane
- Level 26, Waterfront Place, 1 Eagle Street, Brisbane QLD 4000
- ☎ (07) 3223 3200
- britishconsulate@bigpond.com

British Consulate in Melbourne
- 17th Floor 90 Collins Street, Melbourne, Victoria 3000
- ☎ (03) 9650 4155
- bcgmelb@hotkey.net.au

British Consulate General
- Level 26, Allendale Square, 77 St Georges Terrace, Perth WA 6000
- ☎ 08 9221 5400

Canadian Consulate General
- Level 5, 111 Harrington Street, Sydney
- ☎ 02364 3000
- sydny@dfait-maeci.gc.ca

Canadian Consulate
- 267 St Georges Terrace, Pert,h WA
- ☎ 08 9322 7930

Consulate of Canada
- 123 Camberwell Road, Hawthorn, East Victoria
- ☎ 03 9811 9999

Irish Consulate General
- Level 30, 400 George Street, Sydney, NSW 2000
- ☎ 02 9231 6999
- consyd@ireland.com

Irish Consulate
- 10 Lilika Road, Perth, WA
- ☎ 08 9385 8247

hosts

more info

sydney

melbourne

brisbane

perth

web

healthcare

Hospitals & medical centres

For emergencies dial 000. If you need medical advice for minor problems chemists are a good source of information.

Sydney
★   Sydney Hospital, Macquarie Street - 02 9382 7111
★   Travellers Medical & Vaccination Centre - 02 9221 4799

Brisbane
★   Royal Brisbane, Herston Road - 07 3253 8111

Melbourne
★   Royal Melbourne, Poplar Road, Parkville - 03 9342 2800

Perth
★   Royal Perth Hospital, Wellington Street - 08 9224 2244

Medicare

Medicare is the Oz version of the NHS. You will need to enrol at a Medicare office to get your card, and then you can get free hospital treatment for emergencies and a refund on some doctors' charges. It is still important to take out adequate health insurance before you leave the UK. You can call the Medicare Information Service on 13 2011 in Australia.

Medicare offices
★   Sydney Shop 30 Town Hall Arcade, 464–480 Kent Street
★   Brisbane Shop R5 City Plaza, 69 Anne Street
★   Melbourne Ground Floor, 460 Bourke Street
★   Perth Wesley Centre, First Floor, Wesley Arcade, 93 William Street

☺   Health tips:
Sunbathing may be high on your list of things to do whilst in Australia, but be aware of the risks inherent in catching those southern hemisphere rays. Fair skinned people should use a sun cream with a high SPF (25 or more) throughout the day, and between 11am and 3pm the shade is the safest place to be. Hats are always a good option, and to prevent dehydration drink plenty of water.

internet access

Below we have listed a selection of Internet cafes in each of our destinations. Many hostels have Internet facilities and Internet access in public libraries is free. Public Internet facilities are much more common in Australia than they are in the UK and are cheap too – there's no excuse not to keep in touch!

Sydney
- ★ Backpackers World, 212 Victoria Street - 02 9380 2700
- ★ Global Gossip, 111 Darlinghurst Roadd/14 Wentworth Ave/770 George Street - 02 9326 9777
- ★ Internet Backpack Travel, 3 Orwell Street - 02 9360 3888
- ★ Student Uni Travel, Level 8, 92 Pitt Street - 02 9232 8444
- ★ ITAS, 552 Crown Street - 02 9318 1256
- ★ Well Connected, 35 Glebe Point Glebe - 02 9566 2655
- ★ Sydney City Internet, 700 George Street - 02 9211 8554
- ★ Internet Café, Hotel Sweeney's 236 Clarence Street - 02 9261 5666

Brisbane
- ★ Dialup Cyber Lounge, 126 Adelaide Street - 07 3211 9095
- ★ Email Plus, 328 Roma Street - 07 3236 0433
- ★ Grand Orbit Shop, 16/17 Level 1 Eagle Street Pier - 07 3236 1384
- ★ The Hub, 125 Margaret Street - 07 3229 1119

Melbourne
- ★ Cafe Wired, 363 Clarendon Street, South Melbourne - 03 9686 9555
- ★ Cyber Chat, 181-189 Barkly, St Kilda- 03 9534 0859
- ★ Internet Café, 9 Grey Street, St Kilda - 03 9534 2666
- ★ Melbourne Central Internet, 133 Melbourne Central - 03 9663 8410
- ★ Outlook, 196 Commercial Road, Prahran - 03 9521 4227

Perth
- ★ El Nino, Sidewalk Eatery, 207 Murray Street - 08 9481 7204
- ★ Travellers Club, 499 Wellington Street
- ★ Indigo Net Café & Lodge, 256 West Coast Highway, Scarborough - 08 9245 3388
- ★ Global Grapevine, 68 Aberdeen Street, Northbridge - 08 9228 4330
- ★ Net Chat, 196a William Street, Northbridge - 08 9228 2011

hosts

more info

sydney

melbourne

brisbane

perth

web

telecommunications

Useful numbers

Phone kiosks are located in all public areas and hostels.

☎   To call Oz from abroad dial 0061 + area code (drop the zero) + number.

☎   Area Codes: Brisbane 07, Melbourne 03,Perth 08, Sydney 02.

☎   To call the UK from Oz dial 00 11 44+area code (without the first 0)+ number.

☎   To call Ireland from Oz dial 00 11 353 + area code (without the first 0)+ number.

☎   To call Canada from Oz dial 0011 1 + the 10 digit number.

☎   International Operator 1225.

☎   Operator 013.

☎   Local and national directory assistance 12 455.

☎   Emergency Services 000.

Peak call times are between 7am to 7pm Mon-Fri, standard rate calls are between 7pm to 7am and weekends.

Mobile phones

Buying a pay as you go mobile phone can be very important if you are waiting to hear from employers or agencies about interviews and opportunities. The cost of using your own mobile phone on roaming whilst travelling will probably be higher than if you get a pay as you go handset when you arrive.

creepy crawlies

Creepy crawlies

Australia is home to lots of weird, scary and dangerous stuff. Don't let this put you off – incidents of being bitten by a spider or snake are rare. But if you really want to know what's lurking underfoot then read on.

Redback Spider

Australia's most common venomous spider, this little nipper leads to 200 people every year requiring treatment for bites. Symptoms include sweating, paralysis, stiffness and tremors. The spider has a distinctive hourglass shaped mark under its abdomen, and a red or orange stripe on the upper abdomen.

The Common Huntsman Spider

There are two kinds of Huntsman spider, the Common variety, and the Shield. Both live under loose bark, but given half the chance will settle into a house. They are grey to brown in colour with a flattened body. The bite isn't dangerous but the Shield Huntsman's bite can be painful. We don't like this one because it can grow up to 15 cm in leg span.

The Funnel Web

Ah, the world's most deadly spider. How nice. They live in Eastern Australia and Tasmania and like hiding under logs, in tree holes and in your back garden. The body length can go up to 4.5 cm and they are dark coloured. A Funnel Web's bites can cause serious illness and death. The symptoms begin with local pain, mouth numbness, vomiting, sweating and stomach pain. The good news is that anti-venom is available and since its introduction, no one has died from a Funnel Web bite.

★ 9 of the 10 most venomous snakes in the world live in Australia.
★ Box jellyfish swim in the seas around tropical Northern Australia at certain times of the year. Their sting can cause cardiac arrest.
★ What with spiders, snakes and jellyfish, sharks are the least of your worries. (You are statistically more likely to be bitten by another human being than by a shark.)

www.qmuseum.qld.gov.au
www.austmus.gov.au

Poisons Information Service:
☎ 131 126

aussie slang

australia

Banana bender – person from Queensland (we have no idea!)
Bastard – a term of endearment apparently
Battler – someone who works hard on low pay
Bitzer – a mongrel dog (bits of this, bits of that)
Bloody oath – certainly!
Bludger – blagger
Bonzer – great!
Brizzie – short for Brisbane
Click – kilometre
Crook – poorly
Dill – prat
Dipstick – origin of "dippy"
Drongo – idiot
Durry – cigarette
Drum – info, as in grapevine
Feral – someone a bit alternative
Galah – fool. Named after the bird which flies south in winter (when its hot in Oz)
Going off – banging, as in "the party was banging"
Grog – booze
Hoon – hooligan
Kangaroo loose in top paddock – few sandwiches short of a full picnic
Liquid laugh – puke
The lucky country – Australia, presumably for having so many Brits visiting
Moolah – cash
Ocker – pleb
Pommy – Brit
Pommy shower – using deodorant without bothering to shower

Rage – having it large
Rapt – pleased as punch
Sandgroper – someone from Western Australia
Shark Biscuit – novice surfer
Shonky – dodgy
Slab – 24 cans of lager
Snag – sausage
Spunk – totty
Station – a big farm
Strides – trousers
Tall poppies – successful people
Thongs – flip flops
Top end – northernmost bit of Oz
Tucker – food
Ute – Utility vehicle
Wowser – boring person
Yakka – work

Thanks to...
www.koalanet.com.au for their contributions – cheers mateys!

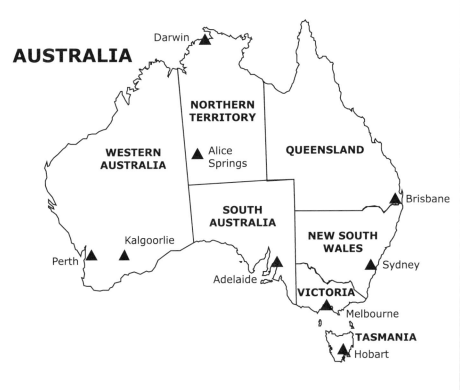

AUSTRALIA

Darwin

NORTHERN
TERRITORY

WESTERN
AUSTRALIA

Alice
Springs

QUEENSLAND

Brisbane

SOUTH
AUSTRALIA

NEW SOUTH
WALES

Kalgoorlie

Sydney

Perth

Adelaide

VICTORIA

Melbourne

TASMANIA

Hobart

hosts · more info · sydney · melbourne · brisbane · perth · web

☺ Safety:

Following the tragedy at the hostel in Childers, Queensland in June 2000, awareness has been raised about hostel safety. Tourism New South Wales issue the following checklist to backpackers looking for hostel accommodation:

- ☑ Are there two escape routes from your room?
- ☑ Is there a working smoke alarm fitted in your room?
- ☑ Can you open the escape doors after hours (night time)?
- ☑ Does the window open for evacuation purposes?
- ☑ Is there an evacuation assembly area for the hostel?
- ☑ Are there loose light switches or electrical outlets?
- ☑ Is rubbish/trash piled up against the hostel?

Source: "Safe Backpacking in New South Wales" leaflet

🕸 www.visitnsw.com.au

walkabout

☎ To call Sydney from the UK & Ireland dial 0061+2+eight digit no.

☺ **Tip:**
During the first half of the week, many youth orientated bars and pubs in Australian cities have "backpacker nights", meaning drinks are cheap, music is cheesy and barbecues are free.

Cool places to hangout...
★ Cafe Amsterdam, 9A Roslyn Street, Kings Cross - 02 8356 9018
★ Coogee Bay Hotel, Coogee Bay Road - 02 9665 0000
★ Home, 101 Cockle Bay Wharf, Darling Harbour - 02 9266 0600
★ Ice Box, 2 Kellet Street, Kings Cross - 02 9331 0058
★ Jackson's on George, 176 George Street City - 02 9247 2727
★ Lord Nelson, Cnr Kent & Argyle Street, The Rocks - 02 9251 4044
★ Rattlesnake Grill, 130 Military Road, Neutral Bay - 02 9953 4789
★ Scubar, Cnr George St & Rawson Place - 029212 4244
★ Watson Bay Hotel, 2 Military Road - 02 9337 4299

Things to do in Sydney...
★ Climb the Harbour Bridge.
★ Look at the Opera House.
★ Visit the Blue Mountains.
★ Take a Harbour Cruise.
★ Go to Fox Studios.
★ Visit Taronga Zoo.
★ Go to Sydney Aquarium.
★ Check out Bondi Beach.
★ Take a stroll through the Botanic Gardens.

To avoid spending loads of money...
★ Walk across the bridge for free.
★ Don't go in the opera house.
★ Take a ferry round the harbour, not a cruise.
★ Eat in cheaper suburbs like Newtown.
★ Don't be afraid to look for less expensive accommodation outside the city.

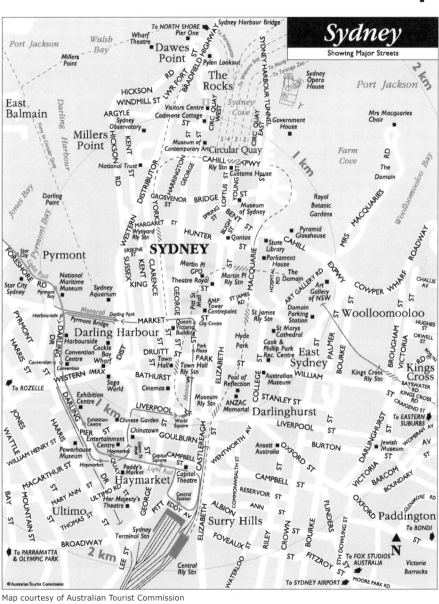

Sydney
Showing Major Streets

Map courtesy of Australian Tourist Commission

hosts

more info

sydney

melbourne

brisbane

perth

web

Get the Card and Get into Fun, Adventure and Savings

Valid for one year, this card will save you money every night you stay at a VIP backpackers hostel.

Plus loads more!!

As you travel, you'll find there's always a VIP hostel in the best locations, offering quality accommodation, friendly service and a welcoming attitude.

There are over 140 backpacking hostels to choose from in Australia and 90 in New Zealand. You will also save on a side range of tours and transport including Oz & Kiwi Experience, Greyhound Pioneer, Australian Adventure Tours, Delta Europa Car, AJ Hackett Bungy Queenstown, Shotover juet and Awesome Adventures, as well as many local attractions and shops. Save on International Phone Calls - Free US$5.

To get your VIP membership card and kit (the kit includes a handy pocket sized wallet with the VIP Australia/New Zealand accommodation & discount guide and a world wide accommodation directory) just visit your local agent or log on to www.vipbackpackers.com

VIP Backpackers Resorts   **www.vipbackpackers.com**

Accommodation

☺ Tip:

If you have a credit card, you can book your first few nights in some hostels over the phone or internet, go to

     www.hostelsydney.com

Bondi Beach

★ Biltmore on Bondi, 110 Campbell Parade, Bondi Beach - 1800 684 660
★ Bondi Lodge, 63 Fletcher Street - 02 9365 2088
★ Sinclair's of Bondi, 11 Bennett Street - 02 9744 6074

City

★ Central YHA, Pitt Street, Sydney - 02 9281 9111
★ Nomads City Central Backpackers, 752 George Street - 02 9212 4833
★ Wake Up, 509 Pitt Street - 02 9262 9705
★ Wanderers on Kent, 477 Kent Street - 02 9744 6074

Coogee

★ Aegean, Coogee Bay Road Backpackers, 40 Coogee Bay Road - 02 9314 5324
★ Coogee Beach Backpackers, 94 Beach Street, Coogee - 02 0315 8000
★ Indy's, Coogee Beach, 302 Arden Street - 02 9365 4900
★ Surfside Backpackers, 186 Arden Street, Coogee - 02 9315 7888
★ Wizard of Oz, 172 Coogee Bay Road, Coogee - 02 9315 7876

Kings Cross

★ Boomerang Backpackers, 141 William Street, Kings Cross - 02 8334 0488
★ Funk House Hostel, 23 Darlinghurst Road, Kings Cross - 02 9358 6455
★ Hancock Hostel, 48a Darlinghurst Road, Kings Cross - 02 9357 2255
★ Original Kings Cross Backpackers, 162 Victoria Street - 02 9356 3232
★ The Globe, 40 Darlinghurst Road - 02 9326 9675
★ The Palms, 23 Hughes Street - 1800 737 773/02 9357 1199

hosts

more info

sydney

melbourne

brisbane

perth

web

work

Office work

★   Assist - 02 9413 2277
★   BOSS - 02 9221 4399
★   Drake Overload - 13 14 48
★   Hallis - 02 9241 3966
★   Hays - 02 9957 5763
★   Integrated - 02 9299 5477
★   IPA - 02 9220 6900
★   Julia Ross - 02 8256 0000
★   Options Consulting - 02 9221 7733
★   Pace Personnel - 02 9299 9909
★   Pivotal - 02 9267 9292
★   Ready Placements - 02 92337544
★   Reddin - 02 9233 7755
★   Strictly Personnel - 02 9413 2842

Accountancy

★   Accountants On Call - 02 2902399
★   Accountants Taskforce - 02 9223 5222
★   FSS Financial - 02 9238 2133
★   Link - 02 9279 1511
★   Manpower - 132 502
★   Michael Page - 02 9254 0218
★   Parker Bridge - 02 9299 9330
★   Recruitment Solutions - 02 8235 9666
★   Robert Walters - 02 9231 3302

IT

★   Hays IT - 02 9235 1844
★   IT&T - 02 9929 7433
★   Princeps - 02 9956 5222
★   Progressive People - 02 9957 1477
★   Talent International - 02 92414545

Hospitality employers

Bars that employ travellers on working holiday visas (WHVs)
★ Arizona Bar, 237 Pitt Street - 02 9261 1077
★ East Village, 243 Palmer Street, East Sydney - 02 9331 5457
★ Forresters Bar, 336 Riley Street Surry Hills - 02 9211 2095
★ Home Nightclub, 101 Cockle Bay Harbour - 02 9266 0600
★ La Campana, 53 Liverpool Street - 02 9267 3787
★ Lord Nelson, 19 Kent Street - 02 9251 4044
★ Mint Room, 53 Martin Place - 02 9233 5388
★ PJ Gallagher's, 74 Church Street Parramatta - 02 9635 8811
★ Planet Hollywood, 600 George Street - 02 9267 7827
★ Watson Bay Hotel, 2 Military Road - 02 9337 4299

Sydney hotels that employ travellers on WHVs
★ Civic Hotel, 388 Pitt Street - 02 8267 3183
★ Dolphin Hotel, 412 Crown Street, Surry Hills - 02 9331 4800
★ Mclaren Hotel, North Sydney - 02 995 44622
★ Merchant Court Hotel, 68 Market Street - 02 9238 8863
★ North Shore Hotel, North Sydney - 02 99551012
★ Stamford Plaza, 187 Kent Street - 02 9023 9624

Agencies
★ Alseasons Hospitality - 02 9324 4666
★ Skilled Personnel - 1300 366 606
★ Strictly Personnel - 02 9233 3226
★ Troys Hospitality Staff - 02 9290 2955

☺ **Tip:**
"Make sure you come to us with all the basics; an up to date resume, references with contactable referees, a valid working holiday visa and a passport. Ideally you should have at least 1 years experience in an office environment and have basic computer skills, including Microsoft applications. You'll be tested on your skills at interview – so be prepared!"
Yvonne Wilson, Senior Account Manager
Strictly Personnel, Sydney

hosts

more info

sydney

melbourne

brisbane

perth

web

work

Nursing

☺ **Tip:**

Some agencies recruit all kinds of medical staff, including administrative people.

Agencies

★ Campaign Nursing - 02 9241 3655
★ Dial A Nurse - 02 9572 9311
★ Drake Medox - 02 9273 0501
★ Gordon Nurses - 02 9953 9388
★ ID Medical Staffing - 02 9957 1166
★ Medical Recruitment - 02 9232 0700
★ Medihealth - 13 2048
★ Mediskill - 02 9267 6500
★ Medistaff - 1800 676 856
★ Nursing Excellence - 02 9552 3975

You will need to register as a nurse at:

🖹 New South Wales State Nursing Registration Board, PO Box K599, Haymarket, NSW 2001

☎ 02 9219 0222

🖱 nursesreg@doh.health.nsw.gov.au

For more information contact:

🖹 State Government Overseas Qualifications Unit, Overseas Qualifications Officer, Ground Floor, 255 Elizabeth Street, Sydney, NSW 2000

☎ 02 9269 3500

work

Teaching

Agencies
★ Drake Overload - 02 9273 0500
★ Select Education - 02 8258 9800
★ Timeplan - 02 9838 0148

Independent schools
☎ Association of Independent Schools New South Wales - 02 9299 2845

For information on registering as a teacher in New South Wales:
⬠ www.schools.nsw.edu.au - New South Wales Education Authority
Contact individual employers for vacancies in independent schools in New South Wales.

Image courtesy of Australian Tourist Commission

hosts | more info | sydney | melbourne | brisbane | perth | web

Backpackers Travel Centre
✉ Shop P33, Pitt Street Mall
☎ 02 9231 3699

Backpackers Resource Centre
✉ Level 8, 92 Pitt Street
☎ 02 9232 7656

Backpackers World Support Centre
✉ Level 3, Imperial Arcade
☎ 02 92235000

Travellers Contact Point
✉ Level 7, Dymocks Building, 428 George Street
☎ 02 9221 8744

If you are a victim of crime or need community advice:

NSW Police Service
✉ Headquarters - 14-24 College Street, Darlinghurst, NSW 2010
☎ 02 9339 0277

☎ 131 444 for non emergency
☎ 000 Emergency

☺ Top travel safety tip:
Don't hang your backpack on the back of your chair in restaurants or bars. Keep any bags under your chair and loop a strap around a chair or table leg. This will prevent it being snatched.

hosts
more info
sydney
melbourne
brisbane
perth
web

walkabout

☎ To call Melbourne from the UK or Ireland dial 0061+3+eight digit number.

Cool places to hangout...
★ Builders Arms, 211 Gertrude Street, Fitzroy - 03 9419 0818
★ Chevron Club, 519 St Kilda Road - 03 9510 1281
★ Club UK, 169 Exhibition Street – Carwash Disco on Wednesdays - 03 9663 2075
★ Esplanade (Espy), 11 Upper Esplanade,St Kilda - 03 9534 0211
★ Great Britain Hotel, 447 Church Street, Richmond - 03 9429 5066
★ Hairy Canary, 212 Little Collins Street - 03 9654 2471
★ Melbourne Metro, 20 Bourke Street - 03 9663 4288
★ Pint on Punt, 42 Punt Road, Windsor - 03 9510 4273
★ Prince Of Wales, 29 Fitzroy Street, St Kilda - 03 9536 1168
★ Roo Bar, Hotel Bak Pak, 167 Franklin Street - 03 9329 7525

Things to do in Melbourne...
★ See the Melbourne Aquarium.
★ Go to The National Gallery of Victoria.
★ Check out the Victoria Arts Centre (next to the National Gallery on St Kilda Road).
★ Take a trip to the high country for the snow (July & August).
★ Browse the Queen Victoria Market (corner of Elizabeth & Victoria Streets) and the Victorian Arts Centre Market, 100 St Kilda Road on a Sunday.
★ Take a tipsy day trip and explore the wineries of the Yarra valley.
★ Visit the Dandenong Ranges for the rainforests.
★ See the penguin parade at Philip Island.

And if you're into sport...
★ AFL Season (July-September).
★ The Grand Prix (February-March).
★ Australian Tennis Open (January).
★ The Melbourne Cup (November).
These are also good times to look for hospitality and catering temp work.

Visitor Information Centre:
▤ Melbourne Town Hall Building, Corner Swanston & Little Collins Street

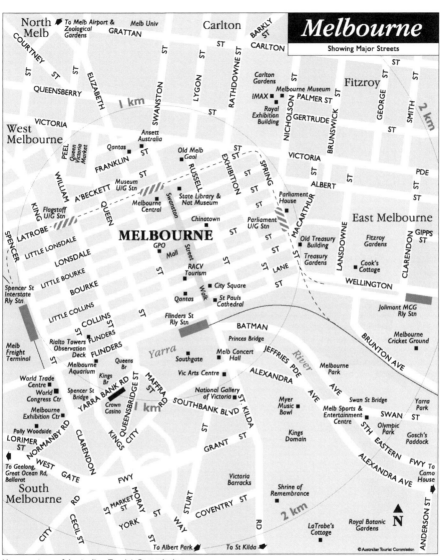

Melbourne
Showing Major Streets

Map courtesy of Australian Tourist Commission

accommodation

Accommodation

 www.hostelmelbourne.com

Central

★ City Central, 475 Spencer Street - 03 9329 7725
★ Elizabeth Hostel, 490 Elizabeth Street - 03 9663 1685
★ Flinders Station Backpackers, 35 Elizabeth Street - 03 9620 5100
★ Hotel Bakpak, 167 Franklin Street - Freecall 1800 645 200
★ Toad Hall, 441 Elizabeth Street - 03 9600 9010

Fitzroy/East Melbourne

★ East Melbourne Hotel, 2 Hotham Street - 03 9419 2040
★ Nomads Pint on Punt, 291 Albert Street, Brunswick- 1800 737 378
★ The Nunnery, 116 Nicholson Street, Fitzroy Freecall 1800 032 635

North Melbourne

★ Bev & Mick's, 312 Victoria Street - 03 9329 7156
★ Chapman Gardens, 76 Chapman Street - 03 9328 3595
★ Global Backpackers, 238 Victoria Street - 03 9328 3728

Saint Kilda

★ Enfield House, 2 Enfield Street - 03 9534 8159
★ Jackson's Manor, 53 Jackson Street - 03 9534 1877
★ Maxim's, 180 Barkly Street - 03 9525 5000
★ Oslo Hotel, 38 Grey Street - 03 9525 4498
★ St Kilda Lodge, 79 Grey Street - 03 9525 4054

Windsor

★ Nomads Chapel St, 22 Chapel Street - 03 9533 6855
★ Nomads Pint on Punt, 42 Punt Road - freecall 1800 737 378
★ Queensberry YHA, 78 Howard Street North - 03 9329 8599

Hotel Bakpak

Abandon all thoughts of roughing it in youth hostels – Australian hostels have come a long way in recent years. A fine example of this is the Hotel Bakpak in Melbourne, which has an in-house employment agency, a café, cinema, lounge area, and it's own backpacker bar featuring DJ's and live bands. You even get free entry into a local gym! The Bakpak group run a handful of hostels along the east coast, all of which have a high standard of facilities. For more info go to

 www.bakpakgroup.com

Office agencies

Office work
★   Adecco - 03 9920 4100
★   Catalyst - 03 9699 1055
★   Centastaff - 03 9330 4566
★   DLA - 03 9670 4244
★   Drake - 03 9245 0200
★   Hallis - 03 96963535
★   Hoban - 03 9203 4900
★   IPA - 03 9252 2222
★   Julia Ross - 03 9602 5550
★   Link - 03 9608 6222
★   Recruitment Solutions - 03 96424299
★   Reddin - 03 9672 6700
★   Westaff - 03 9699 5544

Accountancy
★   Accountancy Link - 03 9608 6222
★   Accountancy Options - 03 9620 9600
★   Balance - 03 9621 1999
★   Jonathon Wren - 03 9963 6300
★   Michael Page - 03 9607 5600
★   Morgan Banks - 03 9623 6666
★   Robert Half - 03 9691 3631

IT
★   Australia IT Jobs - 03 9653 9226
★   Australia wide IT - 03 9321 0109
★   Candle IT - 03 9832 8000
★   Drake - 03 9631 6111
★   Hays IT - 03 9614 7677
★   IT&T - 03 9642 0520
★   Michael Page - 03 9607 5646
★   TCS Computerstaff - 03 9818 0034

melbourne

Hospitality employers

Bars that employ travellers on working holiday visas
★ Arizona Bar, 127 Russell Street - 03 9654 5000
★ Builders Arms, 211 Gertrude Street - 03 9419 0818
★ Box 189, Collins Street - 03 9663 0411
★ Match Bar, 58 Bull Street - 03 5441 4403
★ Melbourne Metro, 20-30 Bourke Street - 03 9662 3798
★ Molly Blooms, 39 Bay Street - 03 9646 2681
★ Studio 54, 2 Queen Street - 03 5441 8711
★ PJ O'Briens, Level 1 566 City Road South - 03 9686 5011
★ The Public Bar, 238 Victoria Street North - 03 9329 6522
★ Places Restaurant and Bar, 24 Little Bourke Street - 03 9665 2666

Hotels that employ travellers on WHVs
★ All Seasons Hotel, 265 Little Bourke Street - 03 9639 0555
★ Rainbow Hotel, 27 St David Street, Fitzroy - 03 9419 4193
★ Windsor Hotel, 103 Spring Street - 03 9633 6000

Agencies
★ Class Act Hospitality - 03 9591 0886
★ Pinnacle Hospitality - 03 9620 9666
★ Skilled Personnel - 03 9924 2424

☺ **Tip:**
"When travellers approach me for work I look for the following things
– they must be well presented, with 6-12 months relevant experience
and a friendly, positive attitude. We will ask them to prove their skills by
completing practical tests. They should be able to carry three plates on
one hand, and know how to pour wine at the table. Grooming tends to be
a problem with backpackers, make sure you have a decent pair of black
shoes and something smart to wear."
Natalie Sixsmith, Staff Services Co-ordinator
LLEM Personnel, Melbourne (now called Skilled Personnel)

Nursing

Agencies
★ Adia - 03 9348 1499
★ ANS - 03 9662 9922
★ BMG - 03 9416 2333/1800 677 948
★ Drake Medox - 1300 360 070
★ Malvern Nurses Agency - 03 9509 8833
★ Medical Personnel - 03 9429 7888
★ Medistaff - 03 9510 1444
★ Oxley - 1300 360456
★ United Medical - 03 9529 3588

You will need to register as a nurse at:
✉ Nursing Board of Victoria, PO Box 4932, Melbourne
☎ 03 9613 03333

Teaching

Agencies
★ BMG - 03 9416 2333/1800 677 948 (recruits teachers and nurses)
★ Select - 03 8663 4755
★ Standby Staff Teachers - 03 9654 7898

You will need to register as a teacher at:
🕸 www.sofweb.vic.edu.au - Victoria Education Authority (for government schools)
🕸 www.sofweb.vic.edu.au/rsb - The Registered Schools Board for non-government schools

For more information go to:
✉ Overseas Qualifications Unit, Level 27, Nauru House, 80 Collins Street, Melbourne
☎ 03 9655 6164

hosts

more info

sydney

melbourne

brisbane

perth

web

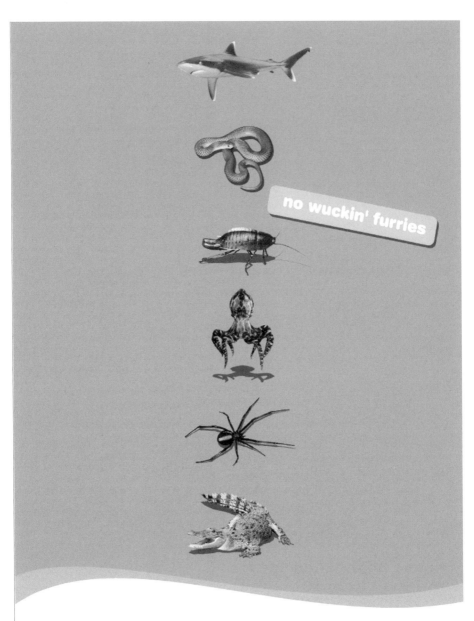

Because you've got enough to worry about Down Under,
we take the pain out of your Visa, CV, Job, Pay, Tax etc.

Call 0208 742 6042
email london@freespirit.com.au

www.freespirit.com.au

Backpackers World
✉ 440 Elizabeth Street
☎ 03 9662 4666

Student Uni Travel
✉ 440 Elizabeth Street
☎ 03 9662 4666

Travellers Aid
✉ 169 Swanston Street
☎ 03 9654 2600

YHA Travel
✉ 205 King Street
☎ 03 9670 9611

If you are a victim of crime or need community advice:

Victoria Police Centre
✉ 637 Flinders Street, Melbourne, Victoria 3005
☎ Emergency – 000

hosts

more info

sydney

melbourne

brisbane

perth

web

walkabout

Cool places to hang out...

★ Brunswick Hotel, 569 Brunswick Street, New Farm - 07 3358 1181
★ Downunder Bar, 308 Edward Street - 07 3211 9277
★ Empire Hotel, 339 Brunswick Street - 07 3852 1216
★ Fortitude Valley is an area of Brisbane with a reputation for excellent nightclubs and alternative bars.
★ Ric's Café, 321 Brunswick Street - 07 3854 1772
★ Shamrock Hotel, 186 Brunswick Street, Fortitude Valley - 07 3252 2421
★ Storybridge Hotel, 200 Main Street, Kangaroo Point - 07 3391 2266

Things to do in Brisbane...

★ Visit Southbank Parklands for "Australia's only inland inner city beach", restaurants and markets.
★ Explore the Queensland Museum in the Queensland Cultural Centre.
★ Mt Coot-tha Botanic Gardens are a good place to chill out and enjoy the views.
★ Go all gooey over the Koalas at the Lone Pine Koala Sanctuary.
★ The Gold Coast (to the South) and the Sunshine Coast (to the North) are only an hours drive from Brisbane. The stunning beaches and scenery make this part of Queensland one of the most popular destinations in Australia. Resorts along both coasts get extremely busy during school holidays.
★ Moreton Bay island is a good option if you want to get away from the hustle and bustle of the Gold and Sunshine coast resorts. Take the passenger ferry from the city for a sunseeking day trip.
★ St Helena island has the remains of a colonial prison to explore.
★ 90 minutes from Brisbane is the Tangalooma Wild Dolphin Resort, where you can whale and dolphin watch.
★ Queensland has a multitude of theme parks to visit, from the wet and the wonderful to the downright weird.
★ Gold Coast
★ Dreamworld, Coomera - 07 5588 1111
★ Seaworld, Main Beach - 07 5588 2205
★ Warner Brothers Movie World, Pacific Highway, Oxenford - 07 5573 8485
★ Wet n'Wild, Pacific Highway, Oxenford - 07 5573 2277
★ Sunshine Coast
★ Underwater World, Mooloolaba - 07 5444 2255

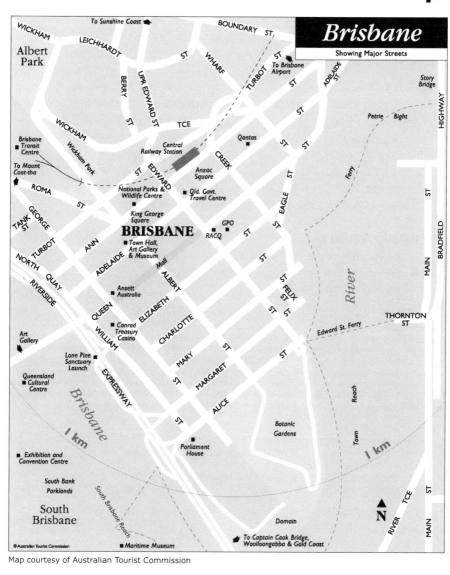

Brisbane
Showing Major Streets

Map courtesy of Australian Tourist Commission

☎ To call Brisbane from the UK and Ireland dial 0061+7+ eight digit number.

Visitor Information Centre:

Brisbane Transit Centre, Roma Street

accommodation

Accommodation

 www.hostelbrisbane.com

The City
★ Aussie Way Backpackers, 34 Cricket Street - 07 3369 0711
★ Banana Bender, 118 Petrie Terrace - 07 3367 1157
★ Brisbane City YHA, 392 Upper Roma Street - 07 3236 1004
★ City Backpackers, Upper Roma Street - 07 3211 3221
★ Palace Backpackers (above Downunder Bar), Cnr Ann & Edward Street - 07 3211 2433
★ Yellow Submarine, 66 Quay Street - 07 3211 3424

Fortitude Valley
★ Balmoral House, 33 Amelia Street - 07 3252 1397
★ Home for Backpackers, 515 Brunswick Street - 07 3254 1984
★ Reefo, 14-20 Constance Street - 1800 173336
★ Shamrock Hotel, 186 Brunswick Street - 07 3252 2421

New Farm
★ Bowen Terrace, 365 Bowen Terrace - 07 3254 0458
★ Brisbane Homestead, 57 Annie Street - 07 3358 3538
★ Globetrekkers, 35 Balfour Street - 07 3358 1251
★ Pete's Palace, 515 Brunswick Street - 07 3254 1984

West End (south of river)
★ Brisbane Backpackers Resort, 110 Vulture Street - 1800 626 452
★ Somewhere To Stay, 45 Brighton Road - 07 3846 2858

Office agencies

Office work

★   Adecco - 132993/07 3000 1500
★   Catalyst - 07 3272 9466
★   Drake - 131448
★   Hallis - 07 336 91511
★   Hays Personnel - 07 3831 5104
★   IPA - 07 3225 7500
★   Kelly - 07 3234 3333
★   Manpower - 132502
★   Ready Placements - 07 3255 2870/07 321 0 2039
★   Recruitment Solutions - 07 3221 1366
★   Select - 07 3243 3900
★   TMP - 07 3226 3066

Accountancy

★   Balance Accountancy Professionals - 07 3229 7455
★   Hays - AP 07 3839 5011
★   KPMG - 07 3233 3111
★   Meritus - 07 3243 3933

IT

★   Ambit - 07 3845 7570
★   Diversiti - 07 3210 4444
★   Drake IT - 07 3291 6099
★   Hays - 07 3839 5044
★   IT&T - 07 3221 9883

hosts

more info

sydney

melbourne

brisbane

perth

web

work

Hospitality employers

Bars that employ travellers with working holiday visas (WHVs)

★ Hotel Carindale, Carindale Street, Carindale - 07 3395 0122
15 mins from city, this hotel also has three bars/restaurants;
Bakers Grill Restaurant & Bar
Finn MacCool's, Irish Bar
Starclub Pokies, Gaming Lounge
★ Adrenalin Sports Café, 127 Charlotte Street - 07 3229 1515
★ Alliance Tavern, 320 Boundary Street, Springhill - 07 3832 7355
★ Casablanca, 52 Petrie Terrace - 07 3369 6969
★ Downunder Bar, 308 Edward Street, Brisbane - 07 3211 9277
★ Hotel LA, Petrie Terrace - 07 3368 2560
★ PJ O Briens, 127 Charlotte Street - 07 32106822
★ Someplace Else, 249 Turbot Street - 07 3835 3535
★ Storybridge Hotel, 200 Main Street - 07 33912266

Hotels that employ travellers with WHVs

★ Couran Cove Resort, HR Dept PO Box 224, Runaway Bay, QLD 4216. You can fax them on 07 5597 9090 or call in Australia on 1800 268726
★ Quay West Suites, 132 Alice Street - 07 3853 6000
★ Sebel Suites, Cnr Albert & Charlotte Street - 07 3224 3512
★ The Carlton Crest Hotel, King George Square - 07 3229 9111

Agencies

★ Catalyst - 07 3216 7709
★ Cordon Bleu Personnel - 07 3221 1722
★ First Hospitality - 07 3257 1844
★ Pinnacle - 07 3220 3244
★ Queensland Hospitality & Security Staff - 07 3257 0020
★ Resort Recruitment - 07 3852 3164
★ Zenith Hospitality - 07 3831 4511

Nursing

Agencies
★   Axis People - 07 3344 1158
★   Critique Nurses - 07 3341 3999
★   Healthstra - 13 1148
★   Northern Nursing - 07 3394 4222
★   Oxley Nursing - 07 3222 4800
★   Queensland Nursing Agency - 07 3221 9883

You will need to register as a nurse at:
📧   Queensland Nursing Council, GPO Box 2928, Brisbane
☎   07 3234 0600

Teaching

Agencies
★   Drake - 07 3291 6099

Firstly you should contact the department that deals with recognition of overseas qualifications, before you can register as a teacher in Queensland.

📧   Skills Recognition Branch, Level 5, Education House, 30 Mary Street, Brisbane, Queensland 4000
☎   07 3237 1900
🕸   www.detir.qld.gov.au/vetinfo/apptrain/skillsrec.htm

In Queensland there are two different boards of teacher registration depending on whether you wish to work solely in government or public sector schools, or in both public and private schools.

You will need to register as a teacher at:
🕸   www.education.qld.gov.au - Queensland Education Authority (for government schools)
🕸   www.btr.qld.edu.au - Board of Teacher Registration for all schools

hosts | more info | sydney | melbourne | **brisbane** | perth | web

Want a working holiday - but don't know where to start?

We can provide you with all the information you need to get a working holiday visa for Australia or New Zealand

AUSTRALIA WORKING HOLIDAY

If Australia is your destination then all you need to do is send an A4 sized, 66p stamped addressed envelope with a short note asking for a form 1150 and we will do the rest. You will receive an application form, a sheet of guidance notes and a free copy of the Travel Australia newspaper. This you will find is jam packed with information on travelling around Australia and New Zealand. It is well to remember that all visas processed by postal application to the Visa Section of Australia House, Strand, London, WC2B 4LA can take up to five weeks.

NEW ZEALAND WORKING HOLIDAY

Should you wish to take a year out in New Zealand and be able to work while you are there, the solution could not be easier. The working holiday visas are available direct from New Zealand House, 80 Haymarket, London. All you have to do is turn up with a passport which is valid for three months after your predicted return date and £30 in cash. The fee can go up or down according to the exchange rate. A word of warning, don't go on 1 September unless you enjoy queuing for hours, as this is the first day of issue for the new annual quota. There are 8000 working holiday visas to go around so there will still be some left months after the 1 September. If you want to make a postal application just send in a SAE with a short note requesting an application form to Visa Section, New Zealand House, 80 Haymarket, London, SW1Y 4TE.

GET A FREE TRAVEL PAPER

If you would just like a free copy of one of our publications then send in the coupon with four first class stamps for postage and packaging. Don't forget to tell your friends about us!

We also offer a wide range of books, magazines, videos & maps. Just complete the coupon below and send to: Consyl Publishing, 3 Buckhurst Road, Bexhill, East Sussex TN40 1QF and we will post you your free copy of our publication.

Please send me a **FREE** copy of (tick appropriate box)
☐ Travel Australia ☐ Australian Outlook ☐ NZ Outlook

Name ....
Address ....
....
.... Postcode ....
Telephone no ....

Backpackers Travel Centre
✉ 138 Albert Street
☎ 07 3221 2225

Centrepoint Backpackers Employment & Accommodation Service
✉ 1005 Ann Street
☎ 1800 06 1522

Student Uni Travel
✉ 201 Elizabeth Street
☎ 07 3003 0344

YHA Travel
✉ 154 Roma Street
☎ 07 3221 2225

If you are a victim of crime or need community advice:

Police Headquarters
✉ 200 Roma Street, Brisbane, Queensland 4000
☎ 07 3364 6464

☎ Emergency 000

hosts

more info

sydney

melbourne

brisbane

perth

web

walkabout

☎ To call Perth from the UK ring 0061+8 + eight digit number.

Perth claims to be the sunniest city in Australia, and its beaches are hard to beat. It makes an ideal starting point for exploring Western Australia in all its glory. You can swim with Dolphins at Monkey Mia, explore the National Parks at Yanchep and Nambung or swim on the reefs of Ningaloo.

Cool places to hang out...
★ The Deen, 84 Aberdeen Street, Northbridge - 08 9227 9361
★ Bog Northbridge, 361 Newcastle Street - 08 9228 0900
★ Bog Fremantle, 189 High Street - 08 9228 3773
★ Church, 69 Lake Street, Northbridge - 08 9328 1065
★ Hip-E Club, Corner Oxford & Newcastle Street, Leederville - 08 9227 8899
★ Left Bank Café Bar, 15 Riverside Road, East Fremantle - 08 9319 1315
★ The Post Office, 133 Aberdeen Street, Northbridge - 08 9228 0077

Things to do in Perth...
★ Scarborough beach is only 15 minutes from the city and is very popular, both for its sands and the nightlife.
★ Spend time in Kings Park, where you can enjoy the views of the city whilst having a picnic.
★ Just south of Perth is Adventure world, a big amusement park with water attractions and bungee jumping.
★ Take a trip to nearby Fremantle and wander round the historic seaport.
★ Check out the bars, clubs and cafes of Northbridge.
★ Take the ferry to Rottnest Island from Perth and spend a day cycling round the island (no cars are allowed on the island) in search of the best beaches, diving and pubs.

☺ **Tip:**
If you do want to explore further afield from the city you will need a car. The desert to the east and Nambung National Park are not easily reachable by public transport.

Visitor Information Centre:
🗐 Forrest Place (Corner Wellington Street) Perth
☎ 1300 361 351

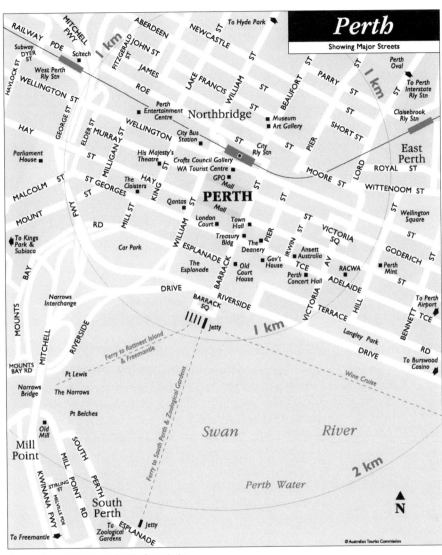

Perth

Showing Major Streets

Map courtesy of Australian Tourist Commission

hosts

more info

sydney

melbourne

brisbane

perth

web

accommodation

Accommodation

⬟ www.hostelperth.com

Central

★ Beatty Lodge, 235 Vincent Street - 08 9227 1521
★ Brittannia YHA, 253 William Street - 08 9328 6121
★ Downtowner Lodge, 63 Hill Street - 08 9325 6073
★ Exclusive Backpackers, 158 Adelaide Terrace - 08 9325 2852
★ Grand Central, 379 Wellington Street - 08 9421 1123
★ Murray St Hostel, 119 Murray Street - 08 9325 7627

Fremantle

★ Backpackers Home, 49 Amherst Street - 08 9336 6773
★ Backpackers Inn Freo, 11 Pakenham Street - 08 9431 7065
★ Cheviot Marina, 4 Beach Street - 08 9433 2055
★ Cheviot Marina, 4 Beach Street - 1800 255 644
★ Freo City, 18 Phillimore Street - 08 9430 5454
★ Old Firestation, 18 Phillimore Street - 08 9430 5454

Northbridge

★ Aberdeen Lodge, 79/81 Aberdeen Street - 08 9221 1666
★ Backpackers International Hostel, Corner of Aberdeen & Lake Street - 08 9227 9977
★ City Backpackers, 156-158 Aberdeen Street - 08 9328 6667
★ Coolibah Lodge, 194 Brisbane Street - 08 9328 9958
★ Indigo Backpackers, 74 Aberdeen Street - 08 9228 0648
★ Lonestar City Backpackers, 17-21 Palmerston Street - 08 9328 6667
★ Ozi Inn, 282 Newcastle Street - 08 9328 1222
★ Underground Backpackers, 268 Newcastle Street - 08 9228 3755

hosts

more info

sydney

melbourne

brisbane

perth

web

Office agencies

Office work
★   Adecco - 08 9461 4800
★   Apex - 08 9288 4544
★   Atria - 08 9226 2200
★   Catalyst - 13 3301
★   Choice - 08 9321 2088
★   Choiceone - 1300 655 060
★   Drake - 008 9215 9222
★   Hays Call Centre - 08 9322 5383
★   IPA - 08 9212 1700
★   Julia Ross - 08 9486 9600
★   Office Angels - 08 9421 1522
★   Recruitment Solutions - 08 9481 2306
★   Skilled - 1300 366606
★   Westaff - 08 9321 4104

Accountancy
★   Accountancy People - 08 9486 1055
★   Hays - 08 9322 5198
★   IPA - 08 9212 1700
★   Professional Accounting - 08 9481 2095
★   Recruitment Solutions - 08 9481 2306
★   Shelton - 08 9324 2288

IT
★   Computing Vacancies - 08 9221 3300
★   E Hire - 08 8211 9600
★   Execom - 08 9429 6040
★   Global Staffing - 08 9382 3571
★   Recruitment Solutions - 08 9481 2306
★   Talent International - 08 9221 3300

work

Hospitality employers

Bars that employ travellers on working holiday visas
★ Aberdeen Hotel, 84 Aberdeen Street, Northbridge - 08 8227 9361
★ Bog Fremantle, 189 High Street, Fremantle (employs Irish travellers) - 08 9336 7751
★ Bridie O'Reilly's, 328 Barker Road, Subiaco - 08 9381 8400
★ Elephant & Wheelbarrow, 53 Lake Street, Northbridge - 08 9228 4433
★ Louisiana's Restaurant, Melbourne Hotel, Hay Street - 08 9320 3333
★ The Lookout, The Esplanade, Scarborough - 08 9340 5738

Hotels that employ travellers on WHVs
★ Burswood International Resort Casino - 08 9362 7524
★ Greenwood Hotel, 349 Warwick Road, Greenwood - 08 9246 9711
★ Grosvenor Hotel, 339 Hay Street - 08 9325 3799
★ Inglewood Hotel, Cnr Beaufort & Fifth Avenue, Mt Lawley - 08 9370 5511
★ Junction Hotel, 308 Great Eastern Highway - 08 9250 1930
★ Sun Moon Resort, Scarborough - 08 9245 8000

Agencies
★ Dunhill - 08 9321 7712
★ Hospitality Total Services - 08 9527 1311
★ McColl Hospitality Staff - 08 9380 4711

Nursing

Agencies
★ AAA Nurses - 08 9325 8100
★ AMA Medistaff - 08 9273 3033
★ Chase Personnel - 08 9481 5200
★ Choiceone Meditemp - 1300 655 060
★ Meditemp - 08 9321 2099
★ NT Medic - 08 8941 1819
★ Oxley - 1300 360 456
★ Perth Nursing Agency - 08 9271 6382
★ Western Australia Nursing Agency - 09 9382 2888

You will need to register as a nurse at:
Nurses Board of Western Australia, PO Box 336, Nedlands, WA 6009

☎ 08 9386 8656

Teaching

Agencies
★ Choice Personnel - 08 9321 2011
★ Drake Jobseek - 08 9221 8377
★ Edconnect - 08 9246 9007
★ Perth Teaching Agency - 08 9448 9256
★ Western Australia Department of Education - 08 9264 4480

You will need to register as a teacher at:
www.eddept.wa.edu.au Western Australia Education Authority
For non-government schools contact individual employers about teaching vacancies.

For more information contact:
Western Australia Overseas Qualifications Unit, 7th Floor, 190 St Georges Terrace, Perth, WA 6000

☎ 08 9320 3747

hosts | more info | sydney | melbourne | brisbane | perth | web

support

Perth Visitors Centre
- Cnr Wellington Street & Forrest Place
- ☎ 1300 361 351

Student Uni Travel
- 513 Wellington Street
- ☎ 08 9321 8330

If you are a victim of crime or need community

Image courtesy of Australian Tourist Commission

australia web directory

Accommodation
www.bakpakgroup.com
www.homehostel.com
www.hostelaustralia.com
www.hostelworld.com
www.nomads-backpackers.com
www.vipbackpackers.com
www.wakeup.com.au
www.yha.org.au

Backpacker sites
www.backpackersaustralia.com.au
www.backpackerstravel.org
www.backpackers-world.com.au
www.backpackingaround.com
www.bugpacific.com
www.freespirit.com.au
www.gapwork.com
www.thewordaustralia.com.au
www.tntmag.com.au
www.travellers.com.au

Brisbane employment agencies
www.adecco.com
www.ambit.com.au
www.diversiti.com.au
www.drake.com.au
www.drake.com.au
www.hays-it.com
www.hwgroup.com
www.kellyservices.com
www.manpower.com
www.recruitment-solutions.com
www.tmpexec.com

Brisbane hospitality employers
www.carltoncrest-brisbane.com.au
www.mirvac.com.au

Brisbane nursing agencies
www.nurseworldwide.com.au

Brisbane tourist information
www.brisbanetourism.com.au
www.brisbotgardens.qld.gov.au
www.koala.net
www.movieworld.com.au
www.seaworld.com.au
www.south-bank.net.au
www.south-bank.net.au
www.timeoff.com.au
www.underwaterworld.com.au
www.wetnwild.com.au

Coach
www.greyhound.com.au
www.mccaffertys.com.au

Currency conversion
www.oanda.com

Driving
www.travellers-autobarn.com

Driving in New South Wales
www.rta.nsw.gov.au - call the Roads & Traffic Authority on 132 213. This site has a useful time and distance calculator for Australian destinations.

Driving in Queensland
www.transport.qld.gov.au - 13 1230

Driving in Victoria
www.vicroads.vic.gov.au

Driving in Western Australia
www.transport.wa.gov.au

Employment
www.jobsearch.gov.au
www.mycareer.com.au

web directory

www.seek.com.au
www.tempsonline.com.au

Flying
www.airnz.com
www.freedomair.co.nz
www.ansett.com.au
www.virginblue.com.au
www.qantas.com.au
www.impulse.com.au

Fruitpicking
www.aaa.com.au
www.employmentnational.com.au
www.jobsearch.com.au
www.madec.edu.au/harvest
www.mildura.net.au

www.waywardbus.com.au

Guide books & text books
www.insightguides.com
www.oup.co.uk/vsi

Healthcare
www.hic.gov.au Australian
Department of Health

Insurance
www.navigatortravel.co.uk

Internet access
www.backpackersworld.com
www.globalgossip.com
www.itas.com.au
www.cafesydney.net
www.cyberchat.com
www.netstuff.com.au
www.theoutlook.com.au

Melbourne employment agencies
www.balanceap.com.au
www.drake.com.au
www.drake.com.au

www.jwren.com.au
www.linkrg.com
www.morganbanks.com.au
www.roberthalf.net

Melbourne police
www.police.vic.gov.au

Melbourne tourist information
www.chillfactor.com.au
www.melbourneaquarium.com.au
www.ngv.vic.gov.au
www.vicartscentre.com.au
www.visitmelbourne.com
www.visitvictoria.com
www.visitvictoria.com/wineries
www.whatsonwhen.com

Newspapers
www.smh.com.au
www.theaustralian.com.au

Organised schemes
www.bunac.org
www.councilexchanges.org
www.travelaus.com.au/farmhost
www.visitoz.org
www.wwoof.com.au

Perth employment agencies
www.adecco.com.au
www.choiceone.com.au
www.ipa.com.au
www.recruitment-solutions.com

Perth nursing agencies
www.wana.com.au
www.oxleynursing.com.au

Perth tourist information
www.bestofperth.com.au
www.streetsofperth.com.au

web directory

www.tourism.wa.gov.au
www.westaussie.com.au

Rail
www.gsr.com.au
www.qroti.bit.net.au
www.railpage.org.au/pass.html
www.railpage.org.au/tt/
www.staterail.nsw.gov.au
www.vline.vic.gov.au
www.wcr.com.au
www.westrail.wa.gov.au

Sydney employment agencies
www.accountantstaskforce.com.au
www.accountemps.net
www.ambition.com.au
www.assistrecruitment.com.au
www.balanceap.com.au
www.drake.com.au
www.fssfinancial.com.au
www.hallis.com.au
www.hays.com.au
www.linkrg.com.au
www.manpower.com.au
www.michaelpage.com.au
www.parkerbridge.com
www.readygroup.com.au
www.recruitment-solutions.com.au
www.reddin.com.au
www.robertwalters.com
www.strictlypersonnel.com.au
www.talent-int.com.au

Sydney hospitality employers
www.merchantcourthotels.com
www.stamford.com.au
www.starcity.com.au
www.starwoodcareer.com

Sydney nursing agencies
www.drake.com.au
www.gordon-nurses.com.au
www.nursexel.com.au

Sydney police
www.police.nsw.gov.au

Sydney teaching agencies
www.select-education.com.au

Sydney tourist information
www.bluemountainstourism.org.au
www.bridgeclimb.com.au
www.cityofsydney.nsw.gov.au
www.foxstudios.com.au
www.scubar.com.au
www.soh.nsw.gov.au
www.sydney.com.au
www.sydney.sidewalk.com.au
www.sydneyaquarium.com.au
www.timeout.com
www.zoo.nsw.gov.au

Taxation
www.ato.gov.au
www.ess.ie

Telecommunications
www.telstra.com.au
www.whitepages.com.au
www.yellowpages.com.au

Tourist information
www.australia.com

Tours
www.autopiatours.com.au
www.backpackerstravel.org
www.contiki.com
www.jarmbie.com.au
www.ozexperience.com
www.straytravel.com
www.waywardbus.com.au

Travel safety
www.catch22products.co.uk
www.fco.gov.uk/travel

web directory

Visas

www.ahc-ottawa.org
Australian High Commission in Canada
www.ausstemb.org.uk
Australian Embassy in London
www.australianembassy.ie
Australian Embassy in Ireland
www.immi.gov.au
Australian Department of Immigration

Volunteering

www.govolunteer.com.au
www.voluntarywork.org
www.volunteeringaustralia.org
www.volunteerinternational.org
www.volunteersearch.com.au

Image courtesy of Australian Tourist Commission

new zealand introduction

Imagine a country roughly the size of Britain but with a population of only 3.8 million. Imagine a country where dramatic extremes like glaciers and sun-drenched beaches, soaring mountains and rolling fields are the norm. This is New Zealand. Combine this with the fact that you can work legally there on a working holiday visa, and you can see why this remote destination is on the itinerary of so many travellers.

If you are thinking of combining Australia and New Zealand, don't spend months in Oz leaving only a few weeks in New Zealand. Allow yourself plenty of time to explore New Zealand, and to make the most of your time there.

New Zealand is primarily known as a place where you go to do stuff. Whether it's skiing, snowboarding, bungee, skydiving or white water rafting, New Zealand is the place to do it. Hill walking or "tramping" as it is known is a great way to explore a true wilderness. Beware though – always find out as much as you can about the walk you are planning on doing. The weather in New Zealand is unpredictable, and some tracks are extremely challenging even to experienced hikers.

The New Zealand winter is from June to August, while the summer season is December to February. The weather varies within these months, depending on where you are. In general, the further south you go, the colder it will be.

Whatever you choose to do, make sure you know what weather you are letting yourself in for, and if you are planning on doing seasonal work, make sure you have picked the right season!

Your first online port of call should be www.purenz.com which is the website of the Tourist Commission. It is a great resource of information, covering all aspects of travel in New Zealand.

New Zealand facts and figures
Summer – Dec/Feb
Autumn – Mar/May
Winter – Jun/Aug
Spring – Sep/Nov

Time difference – 12 hours ahead of GMT. Or in their summertime 13 hours ahead of GMT.

Reasons to go...
★   Landscape - mountains, rainforests, beaches
★   Activities - skiing, kayaking, bungee, white water rafting, abseiling
★   Maori culture

84. *australia & new zealand gap pack*

Working Holiday Visas

TRAVELLERS
CONTACT POINT
AUSTRALIA • NEW ZEALAND • UNITED KINGDOM

Every year the New Zealand government allow 8,000 Working Holiday Visas (WHVs) to be issued to Brits and 1,000 to Irish. The visa quotas are renewed on the 1 July, so if you are applying for one between March and June, check with the Commission that they still have some to allocate. If you send in your application and they have run out for that year, they will refund the application fee.

The WHV is similar to the Australian version. It entitles you to work in New Zealand on a temporary, part time or casual basis for a year.

British and Irish applicants have to apply for the visa whilst they are resident in the UK and Ireland respectively. All applicants applying in the UK need to fulfil the following criteria;

★ Aged 18-30 when you apply for the visa.

★ Not be accompanied by children on your trip.

★ Have a British or Irish passport (which must be valid at least 3 months beyond your proposed departure date from New Zealand).

★ Satisfy the NZIS branch in London that your main intention for travelling to New Zealand is to holiday, and that employment is an incidental reason for the visit.

British and Irish applicants should send a cheque for £30 sterling, their passport, and the completed application form to the following address

New Zealand Immigration Service

▤ New Zealand High Commission, New Zealand House, 80 Haymarket, London SW1Y 4TE

Canadians should apply to:

▤ New Zealand High Commission, Suite 727, 99 Bank Street, Ottawa ONT K1P 6G3

When you arrive in New Zealand you will need to show:

★ A minimum of NZ$4200 (approx £1,300) available funds to support yourself.

★ Evidence of your return or onward tickets, or sufficient funds to purchase an outward ticket (approx NZ$2000, which is about £650).

Application forms and further information can be obtained from

⌂ www.immigration.govt.nz

or from Travellers Contact Point:

☎ 020 7243 7887

✆ info@travellersuk.com

Accommodation

Hostels in New Zealand are often members of the BBH (Budget Backpacker Hostels), YHA, VIP or Nomads groups. BBH has by far the most hostels and their discount card offers good deals on travel too. Otherwise New Zealand has many independently run hostels, some in beautiful locations. Facilities differ greatly, from places that have 10 beds to those that have hundreds. Most will have cooking and laundry facilities (to some extent!). As in Australia, expect to stay in mixed dorms as standard, although single sex dorms can be arranged.

Expect to pay from as little as NZ$20 for a night in a dorm room in low season, to twice that amount at high season in a private room. When booking, remember that peak season is Dec-April, and hostels in popular spots can get very busy. This is also true of popular ski areas in the ski season between June and September.

You can read up details on all the hostels before you head-off at

 www.hostelworld.com or

 www.hostelnewzealand.com

Hostelworld also feature hostel reviews from other travellers on items such as character, location, fun, security and staff. These are independent reviews from people who have stayed in this hostel before so should give you a good indication of the standard. Hostelworld.com feature hostels in all main city destinations including Auckland, Christchurch and Wellington (where it is advisable to book ahead) and also in smaller off-the-beaten-track locations.

A new feature on Hostelworld is the ability to prebook tours and activities online. Check out this service for your bus tours and adrenaline activities in New Zealand. You can do your research before you go at

 www.hostelworld.com

 www.hostelnewzealand.com

Alternatives to hostels include bed & breakfasts (or guesthouses) and camping. Camping in New Zealand comes recommended, as does taking a campervan and using some of the excellent campsite facilities available. Check out

 www.nz-accommodation.co.nz for more camping info, and

 www.topparks.co.nz for site guides.

Guesthouses are usually owned by a family and have rooms for up to 10 guests, usually with shared bathroom facilities. They are more expensive than hostels and are perhaps not suitable for those looking to party the night away!

hosts

more info

auckland

christchurch

wellington

web

Insurance

New Zealand is known as the home of crazy adventure sports. For this reason it is vital that you make sure you are covered fully by your travel insurance policy. If you have an accident, make sure it will be your insurer that pays your hospital bills, and not your family. The following sports are often excluded on standard travel policies:

★　　　White water rafting
★　　　Gliding
★　　　Mountaineering
★　　　Scuba diving
★　　　Skiing
★　　　Jet skiing
★　　　Bungee jumping
★　　　Sky diving

If you are going to New Zealand, chances are you will want to indulge in some dangerous activities. You might like the idea of jumping out of an airplane or leaping off a bridge on the end of a bit of elastic, but insurance companies most definitely do not!

To get a decent package shop around and talk to other people who have been there and done that.

Your package should include medical expenses and repatriation, luggage cover, cash, personal accident and liability, legal expenses, missed departures, cancellations and passport and ticket loss.

Medical insurance

As a rule, if you are a visitor to New Zealand you will not be entitled to any free medical treatment. There is a reciprocal arrangement for UK citizens, but it is limited and you should still get comprehensive medical insurance.

　　　www.navigatortravel.co.uk

hosts

more info

auckland

christchurch

wellington

web

tours

Tours

BACKPACKERS
TRAVEL • CENTRE
www.backpackerstravel.com.au

It may only be the size of the UK but
New Zealand is country that has an immense amount to offer to visitors.
The Backpackers Travel Centre has an office in Auckland solely dedicated
to independent travel in New Zealand and is staffed by people who know
all there is to know about the country.

In the London offices of BTC, the staff are experienced international
travellers and have been around the world themselves. Their own
personal knowledge compliments the content and enthusiasm of the
various brochures we keep in store, and our customers find that this
added personal touch makes all the difference when booking their trip.

BTC works closely with dozens of different backpacker tour operators
and adventure groups in New Zealand – that means that they work with
every type of company you could need when travelling from the UK, from
accommodation and tours when you arrive in New Zealand, through to
travel insurance and visas.

There is so much to see in New Zealand so you'll want to make the
most of your time over there. The BTC Travel Crew can help you plan
an itinerary for all or part of your trip, depending on how long you're
going for, making sure that you cover all of the famed sites in your plans.
They specialise in a number of areas and are fully able to organise the
perfect trip from beginning to end.

Flights are the first thing that you'll think about, and are often the most
expensive part. However, this needn't be a chore. At BTC you can give the
staff your details and they will come back to you with a quote, meaning
less hassle for you! You'll need a visa and travel insurance, along with
somewhere to stay when you first arrive. Through the contacts that the
New Zealand office have made throughout the country, BTC can offer you
a choice of budget accommodation, including budget hotels and camping
villages.

BTC work with a large number of suppliers in New Zealand, whom can
each offer you tours taking you all over the country. Do the "Funky
Chicken" and "The Full Monty" with Kiwi Experience, or the "Grand
National" with Stray Travel or even see the "Top Half Highlights" with the
Magic Travellers Network.

hosts | *more info* | *auckland* | *christchurch* | *wellington* | *web*

tours

A great way to get an idea of all of the places in New Zealand that you might want to visit is to have a look through brochures. BTC have produced a fantastic 70 page glossy brochure "Backpacking New Zealand". This summarises what each of BTC's main suppliers can offer you, how much the tours cost, along with when and where you can take the tours.

To request a free copy of this brochure, please email...
   london@backpackerstravel.net.au
or call free on...
☎   0800 376 1045
BTC's London offices are in Earls Court and Fulham Broadway, so feel free to go along and see them if you'd like any more information or simply want to pick their brains!
🏯   www.backpackerstravel.org

Image courtesy of Tourism New Zealand

Images courtesy of Tourism New Zealand

hosts

more info

auckland

christchurch

wellington

web

organised schemes

A working holiday in

New Zealand
made easy with **BUNAC!**

Participating in BUNAC's *Work New Zealand* programme offers the exciting prospect of working and travelling for up to twelve months on the other side of the planet. Likely to appeal to gap years, recent graduates or those looking to take time out from their career, the programme allows you to spend extended time in another culture and work to finance your travels. Taking part in the odd hazardous pursuit is all part of the experience!

Programme benefits include:

♦ Round-the-world flight ticket valid for a full 18 months
♦ Working holiday visa – we obtain the visa for you
♦ Organised two-day stopover in Bangkok
♦ Group flights – meet fellow travellers before you get there
♦ Support services of BUNAC's subsidiary in Auckland if you need it - for help and advice on finding work and accommodation, travel tips and much much more.

Programme open to students and non-students aged 18-30.
Flights normally run from September to March.

For more information on BUNAC's *Work New Zealand* programme or to download the Application Form, log onto www.bunac.org

Dept. GP1, BUNAC, 16 Bowling Green Lane,
London EC1R 0QH
E-mail: enquiries@bunac.org.uk

Tel: 020 7251 3472

WWW.BUNAC.ORG

organised schemes

Organised schemes

Just as with Australia, there are a number of organisations that provide organised schemes. These are ideal if you are a bit wary of arriving in a country so far away from home without anything definite in place. One of the most well known organisations is BUNAC who operate a Work New Zealand programme.

BUNAC is a non-profit organisation which arranges work and travel programmes for students and young people to various countries. The Work New Zealand programme allows participants to take any job, anywhere in New Zealand. The programme goes beyond the existing New Zealand Government Working Holidaymaker scheme by providing BUNAC's back-up help and support both before departure and throughout your stay through BUNAC's subsidiary IEP. The group flight departures also provide the ideal opportunity to meet with fellow participants.

   www.bunac.org

 ## Case study

Serena Ball spent her gap year on Work New Zealand.

"Aotearoa – Land of the Long White Cloud, or New Zealand to you and me, comprises of three islands in the Pacific Ocean. It is also where I spent 12 amazing months on BUNAC's Work New Zealand scheme. Having completed my 'A' levels, and seen all my friends off to their various universities, 13 hours later I found myself in the humid, bustling city of Bangkok with 24 other BUNACers for two days of sightseeing and shopping. After another long-haul flight we finally arrived at our destination – Auckland. We were greeted at the airport by the friendly IEP rep and whisked off to City YHA, where our first two night's accommodation had been pre booked for us. After the novelty of exploring the city, we slowly began to concentrate on the tasks of finding work and long-term accommodation. I joined up with fellow BUNACer Emma, and pretty soon we had both found jobs and a room to rent in a house not far from the city centre.

January brought our departure from Auckland. Eager to explore more of the country, we bundled our backpacks into "Mitsy" – the classy brown Mitsubishi we had acquired from a car fair, and headed north with Vicky and Kate (yet more BUNACers). We travelled for three weeks; camping in The Bay of Islands, Cape Reinga, then back down through the Coromandel Peninsula and Rotorua to Wellington. We then travelled across the Cook Strait to the Abel Tasman National Park where we were to be volunteer hut wardens for a week. After the week was up we made our way back to Wellington, as we had decided that this was to be our home for the next few months."

getting around

Public transport

Coach

Alternatively you could use coaches run by general travel companies such as Inter City Coach or Newman's. Although both of these companies are national public transport companies, they offer travel passes designed for backpackers and travellers who may prefer to travel with the general public rather than with just other backpackers.

Rail

There is basically one national railway company in New Zealand. The company is called Tranzrail, and the passenger rail side is known as Tranz Scenic. This company goes to a limited number of destinations, mainly taking in the larger cities. However, rail travel can be very cost effective, and while the quantity of routes may be limited, the quality of the routes in terms of scenery and comfort is amazing. The Tranz Alpine trip from Christchurch to Greymouth is rated as one of the world's most stunning train journeys.

Flights

If you are in a hurry to get around, Air New Zealand and Freedom Air have flights between the major New Zealand cities and between New Zealand and Australia. Go to our New Zealand Backpacker Web Directory to check fare prices on the websites of these airlines.

Note:

Don't make a fool of yourself by underestimating the distance between Australia and New Zealand. You'd be surprised by how often tourists ask if there is a bridge linking the two countries! In fact, it takes three hours to fly from Sydney to Auckland.

See the New Zealand Backpacker Web Directory for the links to websites that will help you to plan your public transport.

getting around

Driving

Driving in New Zealand is an option frequently taken by travellers. If you have a valid driving licence and some cash to hire or buy a vehicle, it does give you real freedom. In New Zealand you drive on the left, and the speed limits are basically 100 km per hour on main roads, and 50 km per hour in towns. Be warned that speed limits are strictly imposed and if you are caught going 50 km per hour over the speed limit you will be automatically disqualified from driving. In New Zealand seatbelts must be worn at all times, no matter where you are sitting in the car.

New Zealand's beautiful scenery means that driving conditions can be challenging, and you need to be extra careful on popular tourist routes. The road between Te Anau and Milford Sound for example has steep hills and tight corners, along with many single-lane bridges. In high season between November and March there can be up to 80 tour buses a day travelling on this stretch of road, as well as campervans. Keep your wits about you by not driving when tired or under the influence of alcohol, and resist the temptation to rubberneck the scenery when at the wheel of a car!

Weather conditions, particularly on the South Island can be harsh in winter. Roads will be affected by snow and ice, so be prepared. Have snow-chains for your wheels at the ready, take plenty of warm clothes and some food and drink with you in case you break down and have to wait to be rescued.

 Note:

Remember that there is no compulsory third party insurance in New Zealand for drivers. If you bump another car you will have to pay for it unless you have taken cover out yourself.

Image courtesy of Tourism New Zealand

hosts

more info

auckland

christchurch

wellington

web

getting there

Flights

One of the main reasons that people may decide against going to New Zealand is that from Europe or North America it is a long flight. Not surprising when you consider that the distance direct from London is over 18,000 kilometres! If you go from London to Auckland via the USA it will take roughly 24 hours, and it's a similar journey length flying via Asia. There are a number of things you can do to lessen the pain of long haul flights:

★ Drink plenty of water both in the run up to the flight and when you are onboard the plane. Dehydration can give you headaches and increase water retention, which is what makes your feet swell on a long distance flight.

★ Wear comfortable clothes. The likelihood of a backpacker getting an upgrade is minimal, so don't bother trying to dress to impress! Wear light layers that you can take on or off, and remember that travelling at night is cold. Don't wear anything (including shoes) that fits too tightly or is restrictive.

★ Buy a good rucksack. On a long haul flight your luggage is going to see a lot of handling, so anything too flimsy, or with loose hanging straps will get battered. The last thing you want to see after a 24 hour flight is your underwear scattered across the baggage reclaim.

★ Choose your hand luggage carefully. Remember the bag has to fit either in the overhead compartment or at your feet. Pack a couple of good books. Use the time to reread guidebooks or study maps.

★ Avoid alcohol. Any leaving parties should be held well before the day of your flight, as being hung-over and stuck on an aeroplane for a day is not a good combination. The aim is to arrive at your destination rested and alert, and ready to deal with the challenges that arriving in a foreign country will throw at you.

Read the flights page in the Australia section of this book for more about the risk of DVT and ways to avoid jetlag.

Most travellers arrive into New Zealand at Auckland Airport. It is a half hour drive to the city from the airport. You can get a taxi or use one of the shuttle services, but buses are cheap and run every 30 minutes between the city and the airport.

work

Office work

Employment agencies in Auckland, Wellington, and Christchurch should be able to help you out if you have good skills and experience. To register with agencies or make initial enquiries drop them an email. Compared to Australia or the UK you won't be earning as much, but the cost of living is lower, and there is less competition for temp work than in Sydney for example.

If you are trained in IT, with experience in project managing, UNIX, NT or Java, you will be in demand. If you are a chartered accountant you will also be able to find work. As in Australia, bring a suit and smart shoes to wear to interviews.

How to find the temping agency that will get you working:

★　　Find an agency that focuses on the field in which you want to work.

★　　Read the agencies website and any promotional material to get an idea of their ethos and what they have to offer. Check simple things like how long they have been established, who their main clients are, and how many branches they have.

★　　Email or phone a consultant with any enquiries. Try to talk to other temps who have worked for that agency.

★　　Send in your CV, making sure that you are tailoring it to the requirements of the agency.

★　　Be prepared for the interview and skills testing. Dress smartly and make sure that you have references that are easily checked out.

★　　When you sign up with the agency, read the terms of your contract. Find out what you will be earning on an hourly basis, what you will be expected to wear, what hours you will be expected to work and what your entitlement is to sick pay and paid holidays (if you intend to be around that long!)

Hospitality & tourism

In the major towns and cities of New Zealand, you should expect to find bar work or waiting in all the usual bars, restaurants and hotels. For this type of job you will be earning something in the region of NZ$9 - NZ$11 per hour.

As in Australia, have your black trousers and shoes and a white shirt handy for restaurant work. There is work all year round in city bars, hotels and restaurants. If you want more seasonal work head to resorts such as Rotorua, Nelson's Island and Queenstown.

Ski work

The ski-fields are a major tourist and leisure attraction in New Zealand. The ski season runs from June to October, and interviews for jobs will be held in April or May. You should submit applications for employment in March. The kinds of jobs available include everything from admin roles, to guest services, ski and snowboard instructors and restaurant staff.

There are about 24 public and private ski resorts in New Zealand, the vast majority of which are in the South Island. Some of the most popular South Island resorts include Treble Cone, near Wanaka, Mount Hutt near Canterbury, and Coronet Peak and the Remarkables near Queenstown. These resorts are very popular and extremely busy during high season, so make sure you've booked some accommodation in advance. Tourism is the main source of seasonal employment on the South Island. The two resorts on the North Island are Whakapapa and Turoa.

For information about working in ski resorts contact:

✉   The Ski Areas Association, PO Box 27-501, Wellington
☎   04 499 8135

Alternatively contact human resource departments for the resorts by using the websites featured in our New Zealand Backpackers Web Directory.

hosts

more info

auckland

christchurch

wellington

web

work

Harvesting

New Zealand's largest industry is agriculture, and there is great demand for seasonal workers. If you are skilled at animal handling, sheep shearing or cattle herding for example, you can earn good money. Similarly if you have experience driving tractors or using farm machinery, your skills will be in demand. You could even find work cooking for farm labourers at busy times of the year. There is a lot of general farm work available in the spring, from September to November.

Most backpackers however are happy to pick fruit or hops. There is work available all year long to a greater or lesser extent, but January to March is when a lot of the harvesting takes place for fruit. A lot of plant thinning work goes on in November. You won't earn big bucks – a typical fruit-picker is paid on a "contract rate" by the kilo, and a fast, experienced picker will earn about $15 per hour. If you find work in a packing shed you will be earning about $8 per hour. November to March is the high season for hop-picking, while vineyard work takes place in August.

Selection of fruit farms, orchards & packing houses

North Island:
★   Blueberry Country Ltd, Central Road, South Ngatea - 07 867 7552
★   Bruntwood Apple Orchard, 548 Bruntwood Road, R D 1 Cambridge - 07 8231433
★   Golden Pear Orchard, PO Box 29, Te Teko, Whakatane - 07 322 8245
★   Heritage Farm, Kaipaki Road, Cambridge RD 3 - 07 827 3787
★   Hume Pack-n-Cool, 4 Prospect Drive, Katikati - 07 549 1011
★   Tablelands, R D 1 Opotiki - 07 315 7901
★   Trentham, 52 Trentham Road, Marangi RD 4, Hamilton - 07 829 5773
★   White Cross, State Highway 30, Te Teko RD 2, Whakatane - 07 322 8397

South Island:
★   Clutha Packing, State Highway 8, Coal Creek R D 1 Roxburgh - 03 446 8151
★   Phoenix Orchards, Felton Road, Cromwell - 03 445 1053
★   Remarkable Orchards, Hydromille Road, Roxburgh - 03 4468240
★   Sorrento Orchards, Kinaston Road RD 1 Roxburgh - 03 446 8547
★   Sunbury Park Orchard, 1042 Earnscleugh Road, Clyde - 03 449 2806

Nursing

To nurse in New Zealand you will need a NZ practising certificate, which you get once you have been registered as a qualified nurse. As an overseas qualified nurse, you will need to apply for admission to the New Zealand register of nurses. You can do this by contacting the overseas registration section of the Nursing Council of New Zealand:

Contact Jo Pohatu on

☎   04 802 0243 or

🖱   oseas@nursingcouncil.org.nz

If you are UK trained and qualified as a doctor your skills are in demand in New Zealand. Doctors are likely to want to work on a more permanent basis overseas. The nature of their work means it is less easy to find short-term placements. For this reason, the New Zealand government is tempting UK qualified doctors by speeding up the immigration process.

From May 2002 doctors who qualified in UK medical schools will be eligible for permanent registration as a doctor in New Zealand without sitting the Medical Council's medical registration exam.

For more information contact:

✉   Medical Council of New Zealand (for doctors), PO Box 11/649, Level 12, Mid City Towers, 139-143 Willis Street, Wellington

☎   04 384 7635

hosts

more info

auckland

christchurch

wellington

web

work

Teaching

New Zealand has a shortage of teachers in secondary education. Areas such as maths, science and information technology are particularly under staffed. Around 35% of all overseas teachers in New Zealand are from the UK. If you are a primary school teacher, you will find the most opportunity for work in Auckland.

To apply for teacher registration in New Zealand you must have your qualifications assessed.

Apply to:

  New Zealand Qualifications Assessment, PO Box 5326, Wellington New Zealand

You will then need to register as a teacher by applying to:

  Teachers Registration Board, PO Box 5326, Level 7, 93 The Terrace, Wellington, New Zealand

Every school in New Zealand is run by a board of trustees who are responsible for hiring and firing. Once you have been registered as a teacher, you can look for jobs at

🕸 www.learningmedia.co.nz
and approach the individual school boards for work.

Tax

If you have stayed in New Zealand for more than 183 days in any 12 month period your earnings will be taxable. The current rate of income tax in New Zealand for earnings up to NZD$38,000 (about GBP£11,400) is 19.5%. Before you start work in New Zealand you will need to get an IRD, or tax number. To do this you should call:

☎   0800 227 774

when you arrive in the country. Leave an address, and the tax office sends you the forms. Simply complete the forms and return with a photocopy of your passport, and your IRD number should be with you within five working days.

📖   www.ird.govt.nz

Alternatively you can download the form from:

📖   www.ird.govt.nz/library/publications/geninfo/ir595.pdf

For more information contact:
📧   Inland Revenue Non-Resident Centre, Private Bag 1932, Dunedin, New Zealand
☎   03 467 7020
🖰   nonres@ird.govt.nz

Image courtesy of Tourism New Zealand

hosts

more info

auckland

christchurch

wellington

web

embassies

FAQ

What is an embassy?
An Embassy is a representative office of a foreign country's government in the capital city of another country.

What does an embassy do?
Embassy staff are there in order to promote good relationships between countries. They are there as a "diplomatic mission".

What is the difference between an embassy and a high commission?
A diplomatic mission from one Commonwealth country in another Commonwealth country is called an "Embassy". A diplomatic mission from one Commonwealth country in a non-Commonwealth country is called a "High Commission". The head of an Embassy is called an "Ambassador", while the head of a High Commission is called a "High Commissioner".

What is a consular mission or consulate?
A consular representative (as opposed to a diplomatic representative at an Embassy or High Commission) has less official duties to carry out. A Consulate doesn't have to be in the capital city. The main role of consular representatives is to look after the interests of citizens of the country they represent.

What can my consular mission do for me?
If you get into trouble when you are abroad, a consulate can contact your family or a friend on your behalf. They can help you to transfer money and put you in touch with English speaking doctors, lawyers and interpreters. In an emergency they can cash a cheque for you (up to £100) and make a repayable loan to you to help get you home.

They can't get you out of prison, investigate a crime on your behalf, pay for hotels, legal or medical costs or intervene in court cases.

The key thing to remember here is with a little planning none of this is necessary. Get yourself a decent insurance policy, go to

⌖   www.fco.gov.uk/knowbeforeyougo

and read up about your destination, use your common sense and you should be OK.

embassies

UK High Commission
📧 44 Hill Street,
Thorndon, Wellington

Irish Honorary Consul
📧 87 Queen Street,
Auckland
☎ 09 302 2867

Canadian High Commission
📧 61 Molesworth Street,
Wellington
☎ 04 473 9577

www.fco.gov.uk/knowbeforeyougo
for essential travel advice and tips

hosts

more info

auckland

christchurch

wellington

web

healthcare

Healthcare & emergencies

You don't need vaccinations to travel in New Zealand. What you will need, especially if you are tramping or camping out, is a first aid kit. Make sure the first aid kit contains:

- ☑ Antiseptic cream
- ☑ Antiseptic wipes
- ☑ Bandage (dressing and gauze)
- ☑ Diarrhoea tablets
- ☑ Painkillers (aspirin/paracetamol)
- ☑ Plasters
- ☑ Scissors
- ☑ Syringe
- ☑ Tweezers
- ☑ Waterproof tape

You will also need to get travel insurance with good medical cover. In New Zealand a hospital will treat you for free if it is an emergency brought about by an accident, but in all other cases you will have to pay for your treatment. So get insured!

 Note:

If you are carrying tablets or pills through customs, whether they are on prescription or bought over the counter, make sure they are in their original container.

Hospitals

- ★ Auckland Hospital, 50 Park Road - 09 379 7440
- ★ Christchurch Hospital, Riccarton Avenue - 03 364 0600
- ★ Wellington Hospital, Riddiford Street, Newtown - 04 385 5999
- ★ Emergency Services dial 111

internet access

Perhaps because of its remote location, New Zealand was one of the first places to catch on to the international communications potential of the internet. As a result, most public libraries provide internet access, and there are many cafes where you can send email or surf the net.

Auckland
★ Citinet, 115 Queen Street - 09 377 3674
★ Cyber City - 09 303 3009
★ Cyber Max, Level 1, 291 Queen Street - 09 979 2468
★ Net Central, 5 Lorne Street - 09 373 5186
★ Stages, 62 Queen Street - 09 366 1917

Christchurch
★ Cyber Café, 1/129 Gloucester Street - 03 365 5183
★ Cyber Forum, 143 Armagh Street - 03 366 9445
★ Cyber Pass, 27 Chancery Close - 03 365 9000
★ E-Café@ The Arts Centre - 03 365 6480
★ Netspace Guthrey Centre, 126 Cashel Street - 03 377 8586

Wellington
★ Cyber Centre, Level 2, Breeze Plaza, Manners Street - 04 473 8191
★ Cyberspot, Lambton Square, 180 Lambton Quay - 04 473 0096
★ Email Shop, 175 Cuba Street - 04 384 1534
★ Icafe, 3/18 Manners Street - 04 384 7847
★ Load Café, 115 Cuba Street - 04 384 1871

hosts

more info

auckland

christchurch

wellington

web

telecommunications

Useful numbers

☎   To call New Zealand from abroad dial **0064** +area code (minus zero)+number.

☎   To call the UK & Northern Ireland from New Zealand dial **0044** +area code (minus zero)+number.

☎   To call the Republic of Ireland from New Zealand dial **00353** +area code (minus zero)+number.

☎   To call the Canada from New Zealand dial **001**+area code (minus zero)+number.

☎   NZ directory enquiries 018.

☎   NZ international directory enquiries 0172.

☎   In an emergency dial 111.

Mobile phones

Buying a prepaid mobile phone in New Zealand will help you to be contactable for employers. If you are serious about working and staying in one place for any period of time, try and budget for a phone.

new zealand

map

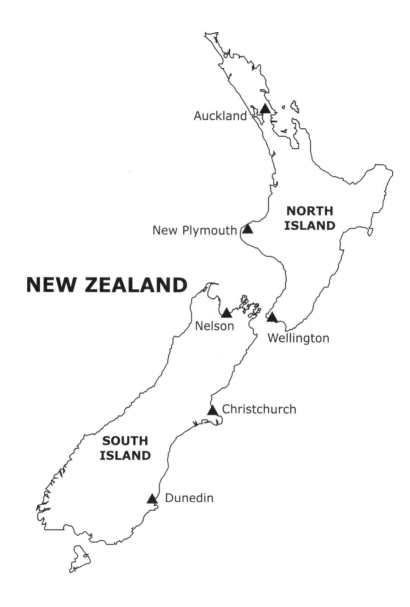

Auckland

NORTH
ISLAND

New Plymouth

NEW ZEALAND

Nelson

Wellington

Christchurch

SOUTH
ISLAND

Dunedin

walkabout

Auckland is a large city positioned between the Waitemata and the Manukau harbours. It is known as the "city of sails" because of all the boats harboured there.

Cool places to hang out (and ask about work)...

☺ **Tip:**
Areas such as Grey Lynn and Mount Eden are "dry" - you can't buy alcohol there!

★ Albion Hotel, Cnr Wellesley & Hobson Street - 09 379 4900
★ Birdcage (open 24 hours), 133 Franklin Road - 09 378 9104
★ Civic Tavern, Wellesley Street - 09 373 3684 (has three bars)
★ Control Room, Queen Street - 09 366 1394
★ Empire Tavern, Cnr Nelson & Victoria Street - 09 3734389 www.empire.co.nz
★ Kings Arms, 59 Frances Street, Newton - 09 373 3240 (has live music)
★ Kiwi Tavern, 3 Britomart Place - 09 307 1717
★ Leftfield Sports Café, Shed 19, Princes Wharf - 09 307 9500

Things to do...

★ Visit Mount Eden, the most prominent volcano cone in the area. The views are great and you can see the remains of an ancient Maori settlement.
★ Visit the War Memorial Museum. It contains the world's largest collection of Maori artefacts.
★ Take a harbour cruise. Going to Auckland and not taking a trip around the harbour is akin to going to Amsterdam and not going on the canals - if you want to go further you can take a trip to one of the nearby islands.
★ Spend a day at the zoo.
★ See a film at the IMAX cinema, The Edge, Aotea Square - 09 303 3345.
★ Buy loads of stuff you don't need and can't fit in your rucksack at Dressmart, the largest factory outlet mall in Australasia, 151 Arthur Street.
★ Sample delectably fashionable Pacific Rim cuisine such as crayfish, green lipped mussels and Kumara sweet potato.

Auckland Tourist Information

▤ 287 Queen Street
☎ 09 979 2333

map

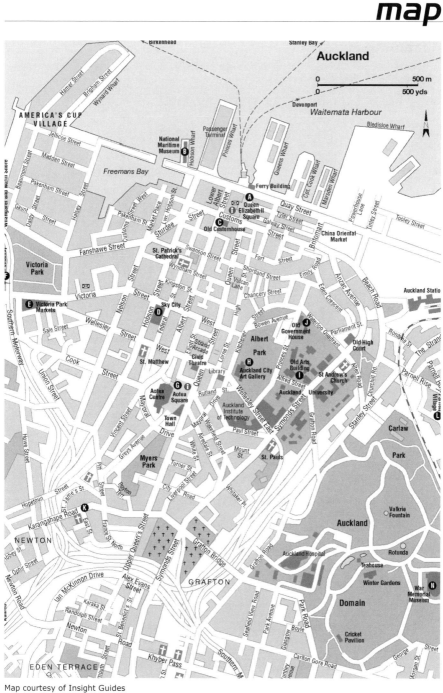

Map courtesy of Insight Guides

accommodation

Accommodation

 www.hostelauckland.com

★ Auckland International YHA, 5 Turner Street - 09 302 8200
★ Bamber House, 22 View Road, Mt Eden - 09 623 4267
★ Brown Kiwi, 7 Prosford Street, Ponsonby - 09 360 1311
★ Central YHA, corner of City Road & Liverpool Street - 09 302 8200
★ City Garden Lodge, 25 St George's Bay Road, Parnell - 09 302 0880
★ Georgia Parkside, 189 Park Road, Grafton - 09 309 8999
★ Nomads City Backpacker Hostel, corner of Gore & Fort Street - 0800 666 237
★ Oakland's Lodge, 5A Oaklands Road, Mt Eden - 09 638 6545
★ Ponsonby Backpackers, 2 Franklin Road, Ponsonby - 09 360 1311
★ Skyway Lodge Airport Backpackers, 30 Kirkbride Road, Mangere - 09 275 4443

Office agencies

Auckland has by far the largest population of any city in New Zealand. The city is spread over a big area, and has developed into four areas that are practically cities in their own right – Auckland Central, which has a population of around 360 000, North Shore city, Waitakere city and Manukau city. Together the greater Auckland district has a population of over one million people. Compare this to New Zealand's capital city, Wellington, which has a population of around 150 000, and you can see why most travellers find work in Auckland. The city's main employers are the business and financial services sectors. Telecommunication companies have expanded in recent years and the demand for skilled web designers and IT professionals is also high.

Office work

★ A&S - 09 837 4220
★ Call Centre People - 09 913 4444
★ Centacom - 09 360 2455
★ Debbie Graham Associates - 09 358 0888
★ Drake - 09 827 8500
★ EVP - 0800 800 387
★ Kelly - 09 273 5577
★ Lampenalectus - 09 366 3866
★ Link - 09 414 4067
★ North Shore - 09 480 2100
★ Reed - 09 915 8900
★ Select - 09 307 2042
★ Westaff - 09 307 2225

Accountancy

★ Accountants Recruitment - 09 309 2623
★ Clayton Ford - 09 379 9924
★ Morgan & Banks - 09 367 9000
★ Quinn Staff - 09 309 8821
★ Robert Walters - 09 302 2280
★ TMP - 09 309 9345

IT

★ Compuforce - 09 379 0672
★ Duncan & Ryan - 09 358 7338
★ MBT - 09 379 0692
★ Pinnacle - 09 361 2750

hosts

more info

auckland

christchurch

wellington

web

work

Hospitality employers

Bars that employ travellers on working holiday visas (WHVs)

★ Alhambra Restaurant & Bar, 283 Ponsonby Road, Ponsonby, Auckland - 09 376 2430

★ Coast Bar & Lounge, Level 7 Hewlett Packard Building, Princes Wharf - 09 300 9966

★ Harbourside Seafood Bar & Grill, 1st Floor Ferry Building - 09 307 0556

★ Jack's n' Juices, 304 Hibiscus Coast Highway, Orewa, Auckland - 09 427 5961

★ Malone's Irish Restaurant & Bar, 6 Miami Avenue, Surfdale - 09 322 8011

★ Mexican Café, 67 Victoria Street - 09 373 2311

★ Neptune Café & Bar, Unit 1, Shed 23 Princes Wharf - 09 358 3118

★ Sahara Tent Café & Bar, 126 Gt South Road, Papakura - 09 298 7775

Hotels that employ travellers on WHVs

★ Auckland City Hotel, 131 Beach Road - 09 303 2463

★ Best Western Mount Richmond Lodge, 676 Mount Wellington Highway - 09 270 2900

★ Carlton Hotel - 09 366 5681

★ The Heritage Auckland, Corner Wyndham & Hobson Streets - 09 379 8553

★ Hilton - 09 357 6442

★ Novotel Auckland - 09 302 9418

★ Park Towers Hotel, 3 Scotia Place - 09 309 2800

★ Rydges Auckland, Corner Federal & Kingston Streets - 09 375 5900

★ Sebel and Quay West Suites - 09 374 2014

Agencies

★ Artisan - 09 358 0500

★ Hotel & Hospitality (HHES) - 09 379 7532

★ Spectrum - 09 357 6442

★ Vital Personnel - 09 522 1961

Nursing

Agencies
★ Acorn Healthlink - 09 630 8300
★ Allied - 09 427 5838
★ Auckland Medical Bureau - 09 377 5903
★ Drake - 09 379 5610
★ Genera Health - 09 916 0200
★ Nurses Society of New Zealand - 09 360 3990

Teaching

Auckland is a good place to find supply work for supply teachers at both primary and secondary level. Elsewhere in New Zealand the demand for primary school teachers has lessened, but in Auckland they are still required. However, the real demand is for secondary level teachers, particularly in maths and science subjects. Listed below are employment agencies that help teachers from overseas find supply or contract work:

Agencies
★ Oasis - 09 303 3616
★ Protocol - 09 307 1203
★ Search - 09 521 8322
★ Select Education - 09 300 7408
★ Teacher Employment Service - 09 479 7970
★ Teachers International - 09 302 5343

hosts

more info

auckland

christchurch

wellington

web

banks

Banks

ANZ
★ 126 Queen Street
★ Corner Queen & Victoria Streets

ASB
★ 120 Ocean View Rd, Oneroa - 09 306 3114
★ 138-142 Queen Street - 09 306 3057
★ 323 Great South Road, Greenlane - 09 571 0272
★ PWC Building, Cnr Wyndham & Hobson Streets - 09 302 1988

BNZ
★ 342 Great North Road, Henderson
★ Level 13, BNZ Tower, 125 Queen Street - 09 3751259
★ William Pickering Drive, Albany

Westpac
★ 229-231 Queen Street - 09 358 2778
★ 79 Queen Street - 09 302 4200
★ Pakuranga Plaza - 09 576 1131

Embassies

★   British Consulate General, 151 Queen Street - 09 303 2973
★   Canadian Consulate, 48 Emily Place - 09 309 3690
★   Irish Honorary Consul, 6th floor, 18 Shortland Street - 09 977 2252

Police

★   Auckland Central, Cnr Cook & Vincent Streets - 09 302 6400
★   Auckland Downtown, Cnr Jean Batten Place & Far Street, Shortland Street - 09 379 4500

Hospitals

★   Auckland Hospital, 50 Park Road - 09 379 7440
★   Emergency Services dial 111

☺ **Tip:**
Auckland Central Travel on Shortland Street help backpackers find work.
☏   09 357 3996

Image courtesy of Tourism New Zealand

walkabout

Christchurch is famous for its parks and gardens. It is also famous for the Wizard, who you can find doing wizardy things in Cathedral Square. Christchurch is the second largest city in New Zealand after Auckland, and is the economic centre of the Canterbury region.

Cool places to hang out (where you can also find work)...

★ The "Strip" along Oxford Terrace is where you can find places for socialising, drinking and dancing.

★ Green Room Café 112A Lichfield Street - 03 365 8275

★ Death By Chocolate, Cambridge Terrace - 03 365 7323. A whole cafe dedicated to puddings and cakes!

★ Café Bleu, 88 Cashel Street - 03 377 2888

★ Chancery Tavern - 03 379 4317

★ Holy Grail Sports Bar - 03 365 9816. "New Zealand's biggest sports bar".

Things to do...

★ See "The world's leading Antarctic attraction" at the International Antarctic Centre.

★ Visit Kaikoura for whale watching and swimming with dolphins.

★ Get hot at Hurunui's Hammer Springs Thermal Reserve.

★ Arthur's Pass is a stunning hour and a half's drive from Christchurch.

★ Mount Hutt ski field is 90 minutes from the city.

★ At 3754 metres high, Mount Cook is the highest mountain in New Zealand. It is part of a huge national park. You can fly over the park and get a birds eye view of the mountains and glaciers.

Christchurch Tourist Information:

✉ Old Chief Post Office, Cathedral Square West

☎ 03 379 9629

map

hosts

more info

auckland

christchurch

wellington

web

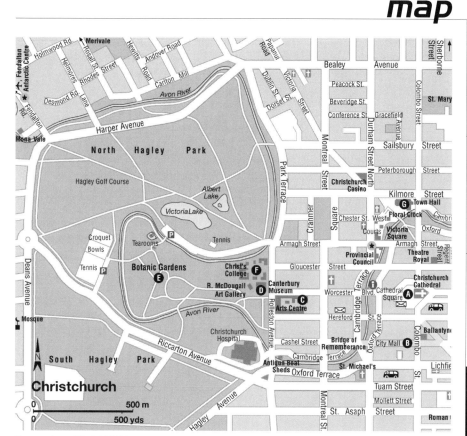

Map courtesy of Insight Guides

accommodation

Accommodation

⬠ www.hostelchristchurch.com

★ Bealey International Backpackers, 70 Bealey Avenue - 03 366 6760

★ Charlie B's, 268 Madras Street - 03 379 8429

★ Christchurch City Central YHA, 273 March Street - 03 379 9535

★ Cokers Backpackers - 03 379 8580

★ Dorset House, 1 Dorset Street - 03 3668268

★ Dreamland Hostel, 21 Pack Street, St Albans - 03 366 3519

★ Foley Towers, 208 Kilmore Street - 03 366 9720

★ Peterborough Guest House, 176-180 Peterborough Street - 03 366 9531

★ Rolleston House - 03 366 6564

★ Round The World Backpackers, 314 Barbados Street - 03 365 4363

★ Shalom, 69 Bealey Avenue - 03 3666770

★ Star Times, 56 Cathedral Square - 03 982 2225

★ Stonehurst Accommodation, 241 Gloucester Street - 03 379 4620

★ Vagabond Backpackers, 232 Worcester Street - 03 3799677

★ YHA Hostels, 5 Worcester Boulevard - 03 366 6564

★ YHA National Reservations - 03 379 9808

Image courtesy of Tourism New Zealand

Office agencies

If you have your own transport and a prepaid mobile phone you will have the advantage over other temp job seekers. Many factories and warehouses are located outside the city, and if you are looking for industrial work, a car would be recommended. Christchurch is known for the amount of call centres that have sprung up recently. You can be paid around NZ$14 per hour for call centre work and temps are frequently in demand.

Office work

★ Adecco - 03 379 9060
★ Allied Workforce - 03 374 9176
★ APS - 0800 365 4322
★ Coverstaff International - 03 377 3992
★ Drake International - 03 379 5940
★ Extra Staff - 03 982 2223
★ Kelly - 03 379 2963
★ Lampenalectus (division of TMP dealing with office support) - 03 374 9222
★ Madison Recruitment - 03 366 6226
★ Manpower - 03 365 6668
★ Select - 03 374 4398 (including industrial)
★ TMP - 03 379 9000
★ TWS Group - 03 352 1002

IT

★ Elan - 03 365 4368
★ MBT - 03 374 8266

hosts

more info

auckland

christchurch

wellington

web

work

Hospitality employers

Bars that employ travellers on working holiday visas (WHVs)

★ Bluenote Bar & Restaurant, 20 New Regent Street - 03 379 9674
★ Bohemian Café & Bar, 256 Oxford Terrace - 03 366 2563
★ Chameleon Bar, 170 Tuam Street - 03 365 5648
★ Clock Pub & Restaurant, Cnr Bayley Street and Main South Road, Hornby - 03 349 3113
★ LA's Bar & Café, 31 Dundas Street - 03 366 6877
★ Lone Star Café & Bar, 26 Manchester Street - 03 365 7086
★ O'Malley's Irish Pub, 480 Colombo Street - 03 379 2098
★ Oxford On Avon, 794 Colombo Street - 03 379 7148
★ The Temple Bar, 39 Dundas Street - 03 377 3175
★ The Vic & Whale, Cnr Colombo & Armagh Streets - 03 366 6355

Hotels that employ travellers on WHVs

★ Carlton Mill Lodge, 19 Bealey Avenue - 0800 422 708
★ Heritage, 28 Cathedral Square - 03 377 9722
★ Holiday Inn, 356 Oxford Terrace - 03 379 1180
★ Latimer Hotel, 30 Latimer Square - 03 379 6760
★ Rydges, Cnr Oxford Terrace & Worcester Street - 03 379 4700

Agencies

★ Hospitality Personnel - 03 329 9900

Nursing

★ Christchurch Nursing Bureau - 03 379 9732
★ NZ Nursing Agency - 03 332 7407
★ Triple O Medical - 0800 150 009

Teaching

★ Teaching Jobs Ltd - 03 326 4203
★ Quick Help Services for Schools - 03 389 1235
★ Capita Education 03 384 7239

banks & support

Banks

ASB
★ Northlands Shopping Centre, Papanui - 03 3432921
★ 105-107 Riccarton Road - 03 341 3064

BNZ (all general enquiries to 0800 275 269)
★ 137 Armagh Street
★ Corner of Cashel and Fitzgerald, 114 Fitzgerald Avenue
★ BNZ House, 129 Hereford Street
★ Christchurch International Airport
★ Riccarton Banking Centre, 81 Riccarton Rd

Westpac (all general enquiries to 0800 400 600)
★ 93 Armagh Street
★ 15 Bishopdale Court
★ Corner of Cashel & High Streets
★ 4 Buckley's Road
★ 1066 Colombo Street
★ 45D Main Rd North, Papanui

Support network

Embassies
There are no consular representatives in Christchurch. See the contacts in Auckland and Wellington.

Police
★ Christchurch Beat Section, Cathedral Square - 03 379 0123
★ Christchurch Central, Cnr Hereford Street & Cambridge Terrace - 03 363 7400

Hospitals
★ Christchurch Hospital, Riccarton Avenue - 03 364 0600

☎ Emergency Services dial 111

walkabout

Located on a stunning harbour, Wellington is the capital city of New Zealand. It is the political heart of the country, and has a tradition of civic pride in its cultural activities. Downtown Wellington is divided into four quarters, each with its own distinctive feel. Lambton and Willis are where you will find more upmarket shops. Cuba has a bohemian atmosphere with markets and boutiques, while Courtenay has enough cafes to keep the most dedicated coffee drinkers happy. Wellington is well known as a caffeine crazy place. Find out why when you sample some coffee at any number of cafes in the city.

Cool places to hang out (and ask about work)...

★   Courtenay Place is the main street in Wellington that is host to lots of bars, clubs and pubs.

★   The Grand, Courtenay Place - 04 801 7800

★   Shed 5, Queens Wharf - 04 801 7800

★   Arizona, Cnr Grey Street and Featherstone Street - 04 495 7867

★   Back Bencher Pub, 34 Moleworth Street - 04 472 3065

Things to do...

★   Visit Te Papa (meaning "our place"). This is the national museum of New Zealand, and is situated on Cable Street, on the waterfront.

      www.tepapa.gov.nz

★   Take a free tour around the historic buildings of the New Zealand parliament, including the famous "beehive" building.

★   Take the cable car through the botanic gardens.

★   Art lovers should check out the New Zealand Portrait gallery, the City Gallery of Wellington and the NZ Academy of Fine Arts.

★   See a real Kiwi at the zoo

      www.zoo.wcc.govt.nz

★   More animal magic at the Red Rocks Seal Colony along the south coast.

Wellington Tourist Information:

      Corner of Victoria and Wakefield Streets, Civic Square

☎   04 802 4860

map

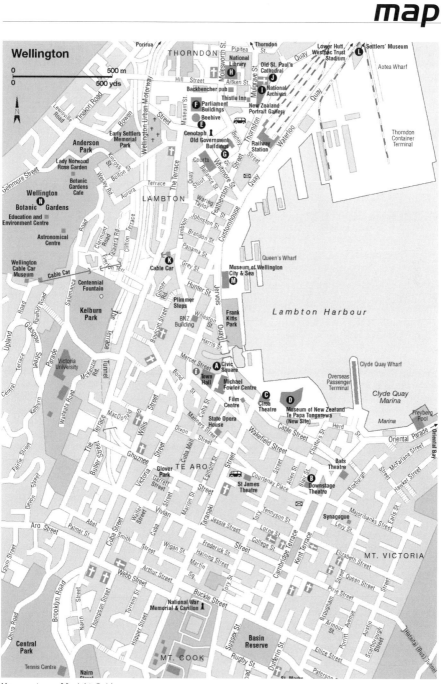

hosts

more info

auckland

christchurch

wellington

web

accommodation

Accommodation

⬠ www.hostelwellington.com

★ Beethoven House, 89 Brougham Street - 04 939 4678
★ Cambridge Hotel, 28 Cambridge Terrace - 04 385 8829
★ Maple Lodge, 52 Ellice Street - 04 385 3771
★ Newtown Heights, 3 Paeroa Street, Newtown - 04 389 8623 (has apartments to let rather than rooms)
★ Riddiford Street Hostel, Wellington Hospital Grounds, 39 Riddiford Street - 04 385 5362
★ Rosemere Backpackers, 6 Macdonald Crescent - 04 384 3041
★ Rowena's City Lodge, 115 Brougham Street - 0800 801 414
★ Trekkers, 213 Cuba Street - 04 385 2153
★ Wildlife Home, 58 Tory Street - 04 381 3899
★ Worldwide Lodge, 291 The Terrace - 04 802 5390
★ YHA Wellington, 292 Wakefield Street - 04 801 7280

Office agencies

Wellington has many major companies who recruit temps regularly. If you wanted to work with a particular company, you could try finding their website and contacting their human resources department directly.

     www.workingin.com
has listings of large employers in New Zealand. Alternatively you could contact one of the agencies listed below. Depending on your skills and experience expect to earn between NZ$10 – NZ$17 in an office support role. IT and accounting people will earn more.

June and July tend to be better for temp work, Christmas is pretty quiet.

Wellington is the centre for banking and government departments, so there is demand for admin and financial staff.

General & financial
★   Adecco - 04 472 9115
★   Drake International - 04 472 6972
★   Kelly - 04 499 2825
★   Lampenelectus (division of TMP dealing with office support) - 04 473 4033
★   MBT - 04 498 0500
★   Select - 04 9166 740
★   TMP - 04 498 0770
★   Westaff - 04 473 4361

IT
★   Diversiti - 04 471 1530
★   Duncan & Ryan - 04 802 4888
★   MBT - 04 498 0500
★   Mercury 04 499 2624

☺   **Tip:**
"Employment agencies in New Zealand like using travellers as temps because they tend to be degree educated and have specialist backgrounds. Any technical ability and skills are highly sought after. If you have a working holiday visa for Australia and New Zealand, and register with an agency that has branches in both, you can save time by having your registration transferred between the offices in each country."
Cara Bartley, Recruitment Executive
Select Appointments New Zealand

hosts
more info
auckland
christchurch
wellington
web

work

Hospitality employers

Bars that employ travellers on working holiday visas (WHVs)

★ Cobar Bar & Restaurant, 12 Main Street, Days Bay, Lower Hutt - 04 939 4133

★ Danny Boy's Irish Tavern, 72 High Street, Lower Hutt - 04 939 4133

★ Eden Wharf, Greta Point Wharf, Evans Bay - 04 386 1363

★ Giuliani's Bar & Grill, 290 Wakefield Street, Courtney Place - 04 803 3303

★ Logan Brown, 192 Cuba Street - 04 801 5114

★ Molly Malone's, Cnr Taranaki Street & Courtenay Place - 04 384 2896

★ Sandbar Pub, 103 Mana Esplanade, Mana - 04 233 1397

★ The Opera Restaurant & Bar, Cnr Courtenay Place & Blair Street - 04 382 8654

Hotels that employ travellers on WHVs

★ Bay Plaza, 40-44 Oriental Parade - 04 385 7799

★ Brentwood Hotel, 16 Kemp Street, Kilbirnie - 04 920 0400

★ Central City Apartment, 130 Victoria Street - 04 385 4166

★ Museum Hotel, 90 Cable Street - 04 802 8900

★ West Plaza Hotel, 110–116 Wakefield Street - 04 473 1440

Agencies

★ Red Herring Catering - 04 4788 700

Nursing

★ Duty Calls - 04 381 8666

★ Care Direct - 04 499 0081

★ Neighbourhood Nurses - 04 904 9899

★ Healthcare NZ - 04 298 9922

★ Homecare 2000 - 04 570 0662

★ The Nursing Trust - 04 569 4750

Teaching

★ Education Personnel - 04 387 9988

Banks

ANZ
★ 86-90 Lambton Quay - 0800 180923
★ 107-109 Queens Drive, Lower Hutt - 0800 180 920
★ Corner Queen & George Streets - 0800 180927

ASB
★ Level 1, 138 The Square, Palmerston North - 0800 787 252
★ Shop 47, Westfield Shoppingtown, 34 Johnsonville Road - 04 477 5000
★ 29 Manners Street, Wellington Central - 04 472 5391
★ NCR House, 342-352 Lambton Quay - 04 494 1850
★ 198 Lambton Quay - 04 499 0864
★ 195 High Street, Lower Hutt - 04 560 9152

BNZ (all general enquiries 0800 2400 00)
★ State Insurance Tower, 1 Willis Street
★ 222 Lambton Quay
★ 50 Manners Street

Westpac (all general enquiries 0800 400 600)
★ 318 Lambton Quay
★ 160 Adelaide Road
★ 119-125 Willis Street
★ 10-14 Courtney Place
★ 74-76 Cuba Street
★ 31-33 Ghuznee Street

hosts

more info

auckland

christchurch

wellington

web

Embassies

★ British High Commission, 44 Hill Street, Wellington - 04 924 2888
★ Canadian High Commission, 3rd Floor, 61 Molesworth Street, Thorndon, Wellington - 04 473 9577

Police

★ District HQ, Corner Victoria & Harris Streets - 04 381 2000
★ Emergency Services dial 111

Hospitals

★ Wellington Hospital, Riddiford Street, Newtown - 04 385 5999
★ Emergency Services dial 111

Image courtesy of Tourism New Zealand

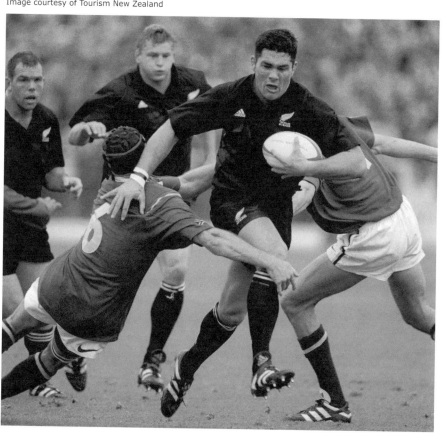

hosts

more info

auckland

christchurch

wellington

web

web directory

Accommodation
www.bbh.co.nz
www.backpack.co.nz
www.hostelnewzealand.com
www.vip.co.nz
www.yha.org.nz

Accountancy recruitment
www.ambitionconnect.com.au
www.arthurandersen.com
www.employment.byron.com.au
www.hays-ap.com
www.kpmg.co.nz
www.monster.com.au

Activity guides
www.alpinerecreation.co.nz
www.blackwaterrafting.co.nz
www.canterburycat.co.nz
www.divenewzealand.com
www.divenz.com
www.diving.co.nz
www.dolphinswim.co.nz
www.newzealandsearch.co.nz
www.nzsafaris.co.nz
www.rivervalley.co.nz

Auckland
www.akcity.govt.nz
www.akmuseum.org.nz
www.aucklandnz.com
www.aucklandzoo.co.nz
www.herald.co.nz
www.nzcity.co.nz

Backpacker sites
www.backpackerstravel.org
www.gapwork.com
www.freespirit.com.au
www.lonelyplanet.com
For more see the Australia Web
Directory

Banks
www.anz.co.nz
www.asbbank.co.nz
www.bnz.co.nz
www.westpac.co.nz

Christchurch
www.christchurch.nz.net

Currency conversion
www.oanda.com

Embassies
Email the Canadian embassy on
wlgtn@dfait-maeci.gc.ca
www.britain.org.nz
www.ireland.co.nz

Employment agencies
www.dgal.co.nz
www.manpower.co.nz
www.michaelpage.com.au
www.momentum.co.nz
www.people.co.nz
www.robertwalters.com

Flying
www.airnz.com
www.freedomair.co.nz

Fruitpicking
www.farmnews.co.nz
www.hortnet.co.nz
www.maf.govt.nz
www.nzhops.co.nz
www.seasonalwork.co.nz

General jobsearch
www.careers.co.nz
www.monster.co.nz
www.nzjobs.co.nz
www.nzjobs.co.nz
www.queenstownonline.co.nz/
addstaff
www.winz.govt.nz

web directory

www.workingin.com
www.workingin.com

Guide books & text books
www.insightguides.com
www.oup.co.uk/vsi

Healthcare
www.adbh.govt.nz
www.hospitals.co.nz
www.wnhealth.co.nz

Hospitality recruitment
www.artisan-recruitment.com
www.hhes.co.nz
www.mall.co.nz/hospjobs/
www.traveljobs.co.nz

Insurance
www.navigatortravel.co.uk

IT recruitment
www.candle.co.nz
www.diversiti.co.nz
www.itfutures.co.nz
www.southern-alps.com

Maps online
www.mapquest.com
www.maps.com

New Zealand tourist information
www.purenz.com

Newspapers
www.nzherald.com

Nursing
www.hospitals.co.nz
www.mcnz.org.nz
www.moh.govt.nz

www.nursingcouncil.org.nz
www.nursingnz.co.nz
www.nznursing.co.nz
www.southerndoctor.co.nz

Organised schemes
www.bunac.org

Public transport
www.intercitycoach.co.nz
www.newmanscoach.co.nz

Ski work
www.goski.com
www.new-zealand.com/TrebleCone/jobs.html
www.nzski.com

Taxation
www.ess.ie
www.ird.govt.nz

Teaching
www.edgazette.govt.nz
www.edna.edu.au
www.nz-education.com
www.teacheremployment.com.au
www.teachersonthemove.com
www.teachnz.govt.nz

Telecommunications
www.whitepages.co.nz
www.yellowpages.co.nz

Tours
www.contiki.com
www.kiwiexperience.com
www.magicbus.co.nz
www.straytravel.com

Travel safety
www.catch22products.co.uk
www.fco.gov.uk/travel

hosts

more info

auckland

christchurch

wellington

web

web directory

Visas
www.immigration.govt.nz
www.travellers.com.au

Weather
www.bom.gov.au

www.metservice.co.nz

Wellington
www.experiencenz.com
www.searchwellington.co.nz
www.wellingtonnz.com

Image courtesy of Tourism New Zealand

the
gap year
diary

The Gapwork Gap Year diary is a great way of recording your experiences during your year out.

It is designed to help you to reflect on what you have done, record when you did it, and think through how the experience will be of benefit to you.

We don't expect you to spend time every day writing detailed notes about every train you caught or mountain you climbed. Instead, we have allocated a page per week of your year out. This is just enough space to enter the date, where you were, what you did, and how it affected you. Remember that the end goal of your year out is to build skills, and to develop as an individual. During your gap year you can:

- ★ Build your self confidence
- ★ Develop your communication skills
- ★ Become more self aware
- ★ Set yourself new challenges
- ★ Prove that you are adaptable
- ★ Learn to work on your own initiative
- ★ Develop your team building skills

Aim to use your experiences to achieve the things listed above.

 www.oup.co.uk/vsi

If you are taking a year out between school and university, it is important to bear your studies in mind while you are travelling. Whether you've secured a place on a course or not, it will help you settle into your studies if you have done some reading in advance.

If you are doing a degree in a subject that is new to you, you'll benefit from reading up about the subject before starting university. Oxford University Press publish a great range of books called "A Very Short Introduction To..." The series encompasses everything from Ancient Philosophy to Twentieth Century Britain, and will help you to get your head around some tricky degree level subjects without feeling like you're back in school. Each book is only about 100 pages long, and is a handy pocket size, ideal for carrying around with you on your travels. Just think – you could brush up on your politics or quantum theory while sunbathing on an Aussie beach!

The books are also ideal for anyone returning from their travels with time to kill at home before their course begins. "A Very Short Introduction To..." gives you an insight into a subject without overwhelming you with information. You'll have years to get the details of a subject at university, what you need at this early stage is a starting point. This is what the series aims to provide.

Gap year travelling should be about taking a journey in every sense of the word – physically and mentally. When you come home, you should be more mature, confident and ready to tackle all the challenges that university life can throw at you. Brushing up on your studies whilst you are on your year out will help you to settle into uni life, and give you the confidence to make the most of your degree.

So while you are travelling, try to take time out of every day to reflect on your experiences. Read a little, think about how what you are doing relates to what you will be doing when you get home. Make notes in your gap year diary and in any books you take with you to help you read up about your degree subject.

     www.oup.co.uk/vsi

week I: date -

diary

Where I went:

What I did:

People I met:

Email addresses:

Phone numbers:

High point:

What I learnt about myself:

Budget:

	cash	credit card	debit card	travellers cheques
Accom				
Travel				
Food				
Drink				
Socialising				

☺ **Work tip:**
"When you arrive in Sydney, or any other Australian city, develop relationships with three employment agencies who seem most useful for you. Keep them up to date with your availability to work and any sudden changes in plans you may have."
Maria Kehagias, Senior Recruitment Consultant
IPA Personnel, Sydney

week 2: date -

Where I went:

What I did:

People I met:

Email addresses:

Phone numbers:

High point:

What I learnt about myself:

Budget:

	cash	credit card	debit card	travellers cheques
Accom				
Travel				
Food				
Drink				
Socialising				

week 3: date -

Where I went:

What I did:

People I met:

Email addresses:

Phone numbers:

High point:

What I learnt about myself:

Budget:

	cash	credit card	debit card	travellers cheques
Accom				
Travel				
Food				
Drink				
Socialising				

week 4: date -

Where I went:

What I did:

People I met:

Email addresses:

Phone numbers:

High point:

What I learnt about myself:

Budget:

	cash	credit card	debit card	travellers cheques
Accom				
Travel				
Food				
Drink				
Socialising				

Did you know?

Australia is the sixth largest country in the world, but has the world's lowest population density – only two people per square kilometre.

 www.australia.com

week 5: date -

diary

Where I went:

What I did:

People I met:

Email addresses:

Phone numbers:

High point:

What I learnt about myself:

Budget:

	cash	credit card	debit card	travellers cheques
Accom				
Travel				
Food				
Drink				
Socialising				

🐑 **Quote:**

"A gap year is an opportunity to gain more independence…(and)… meet people from different backgrounds and cultures."

Marks and Spencer Graduate Recruitment

 www.marksandspencer.com/opportunities

week 6: date -

Where I went:

What I did:

People I met:

Email addresses:

Phone numbers:

High point:

What I learnt about myself:

Budget:

	cash	credit card	debit card	travellers cheques
Accom				
Travel				
Food				
Drink				
Socialising				

week 7: date -

diary

Where I went:

What I did:

People I met:

Email addresses:

Phone numbers:

High point:

What I learnt about myself:

Budget:

	cash	credit card	debit card	travellers cheques
Accom				
Travel				
Food				
Drink				
Socialising				

week 8: date -

Where I went:

What I did:

People I met:

Email addresses:

Phone numbers:

High point:

What I learnt about myself:

Budget:

	cash	credit card	debit card	travellers cheques
Accom				
Travel				
Food				
Drink				
Socialising				

✗ Remember...

You only get one shot at a working holiday visa. Once you've got one, that's it for the rest of your life. So don't waste it! Don't apply for one without being 100% committed to using it.

week 9: date -

diary

Where I went:

What I did:

People I met:

Email addresses:

Phone numbers:

High point:

What I learnt about myself:

Budget:

	cash	credit card	debit card	travellers cheques
Accom				
Travel				
Food				
Drink				
Socialising				

☺ **Travel tip:**

Before you go away, photocopy all your important documents – passport, insurance, driving licence, visas, traveller's cheque numbers and tickets. Leave copies at home with a friend or family member, and take copies with you (keep separately to the real thing!)

 www.catch22products.co.uk

week 10: date -

Where I went:

What I did:

People I met:

Email addresses:

Phone numbers:

High point:

What I learnt about myself:

Budget:

	cash	credit card	debit card	travellers cheques
Accom				
Travel				
Food				
Drink				
Socialising				

week II: date -

Where I went:

What I did:

People I met:

Email addresses:

Phone numbers:

High point:

What I learnt about myself:

Budget:

	cash	credit card	debit card	travellers cheques
Accom				
Travel				
Food				
Drink				
Socialising				

week 12: date -

Where I went:

What I did:

People I met:

Email addresses:

Phone numbers:

High point:

What I learnt about myself:

Budget:

	cash	credit card	debit card	travellers cheques
Accom				
Travel				
Food				
Drink				
Socialising				

diary

Where I went:

What I did:

People I met:

Email addresses:

Phone numbers:

High point:

What I learnt about myself:

Budget:

	cash	credit card	debit card	travellers cheques
Accom				
Travel				
Food				
Drink				
Socialising				

Did you know?

The cost of living in Australia and New Zealand is generally less than in the UK and Ireland. For food essentials expect to pay around one Australian dollar for a bag of pasta or a litre of cola drink, two Australian dollars for a litre of milk, a loaf of bread or a box of teabags, and only twenty four Australian dollars for twelve bottles of beer! Supermarket prices are particularly good value.

A
VERY SHORT INTRODUCTION TO . . .

FORTHCOMING TITLES MAY 2003

EVOLUTION

SCHIZOPHRENIA

CAPITALISM

PREHISTORY

DADA AND SURREALISM

COLD WAR

MYTH

CHAOS

INTERNATIONAL RELATIONS

BRITISH POLITICS

OXFORD
UNIVERSITY PRESS

See page 179 for an exclusive special offer

diary

Where I went:

What I did:

People I met:

Email addresses:

Phone numbers:

High point:

What I learnt about myself:

Budget:

	cash	credit card	debit card	travellers cheques
Accom				
Travel				
Food				
Drink				
Socialising				

week 15: date -

Where I went:

What I did:

People I met:

Email addresses:

Phone numbers:

High point:

What I learnt about myself:

Budget:

	cash	credit card	debit card	travellers cheques
Accom				
Travel				
Food				
Drink				
Socialising				

☺ **Safety tip:**

Wherever you come from, there will be areas of nearby towns or cities that you would be extra careful in. You would avoid walking there alone at night, being drunk, or getting lost. You should approach every new destination with just as much caution. Find out about levels of safety in particular countries by going to...

 www.fco.gov.uk/travel

diary

Where I went:

What I did:

People I met:

Email addresses:

Phone numbers:

High point:

What I learnt about myself:

Budget:

	cash	credit card	debit card	travellers cheques
Accom				
Travel				
Food				
Drink				
Socialising				

Quote:

Advice for working holidaymakers?
"Be keen, enthusiastic, honest and hardworking and your bosses will love you!"
Russell Durnell, Sales and Marketing Director, W Hotel, Sydney

week 17: date -

Where I went:

What I did:

People I met:

Email addresses:

Phone numbers:

High point:

What I learnt about myself:

Budget:

	cash	credit card	debit card	travellers cheques
Accom				
Travel				
Food				
Drink				
Socialising				

diary

Where I went:

What I did:

People I met:

Email addresses:

Phone numbers:

High point:

What I learnt about myself:

Budget:

	cash	credit card	debit card	travellers cheques
Accom				
Travel				
Food				
Drink				
Socialising				

week 19: date -

Where I went:

What I did:

People I met:

Email addresses:

Phone numbers:

High point:

What I learnt about myself:

Budget:

	cash	credit card	debit card	travellers cheques
Accom				
Travel				
Food				
Drink				
Socialising				

✎　　Remember...

School holidays in Australia are around mid-December to the end of January, at the end of September and two weeks in July. This is good if you are looking for work in the tourism industry at these times of year. However, its not so good if you are trying to get into theme parks or book accommodation!

week 20: date -

diary

Where I went:

What I did:

People I met:

Email addresses:

Phone numbers:

High point:

What I learnt about myself:

Budget:

	cash	credit card	debit card	travellers cheques
Accom				
Travel				
Food				
Drink				
Socialising				

☺ **Travel tip:**
You can also scan travel documents and save them on your email account if you need to access them in the event of the originals being lost or stolen.

 www.catch22products.co.uk

week 21: date -

Where I went:

What I did:

People I met:

Email addresses:

Phone numbers:

High point:

What I learnt about myself:

Budget:

	cash	credit card	debit card	travellers cheques
Accom				
Travel				
Food				
Drink				
Socialising				

week 22: date -

Where I went:

What I did:

People I met:

Email addresses:

Phone numbers:

High point:

What I learnt about myself:

Budget:

	cash	credit card	debit card	travellers cheques
Accom				
Travel				
Food				
Drink				
Socialising				

week 23: date -

Where I went:

What I did:

People I met:

Email addresses:

Phone numbers:

High point:

What I learnt about myself:

Budget:

	cash	credit card	debit card	travellers cheques
Accom				
Travel				
Food				
Drink				
Socialising				

☺ **Work tip:**

If you want to improve your chances of finding bar work, get your Responsible Service of Alcohol certificate while you are in Sydney. Take a look at the course offered on

    www.alexbeaumont.com

Where I went:

What I did:

People I met:

Email addresses:

Phone numbers:

High point:

What I learnt about myself:

Budget:

	cash	credit card	debit card	travellers cheques
Accom				
Travel				
Food				
Drink				
Socialising				

☺ **Safety tip:**
Always let your friends, family and travelling companions know where you are, and where you expect to be the next time you contact them. This is particularly important when you are travelling in the Australian outback or tramping in New Zealand.

week 25: date -

Where I went:

What I did:

People I met:

Email addresses:

Phone numbers:

High point:

What I learnt about myself:

Budget:

	cash	credit card	debit card	travellers cheques
Accom				
Travel				
Food				
Drink				
Socialising				

diary

Where I went:

What I did:

People I met:

Email addresses:

Phone numbers:

High point:

What I learnt about myself:

Budget:

	cash	credit card	debit card	travellers cheques
Accom				
Travel				
Food				
Drink				
Socialising				

week 27: date -

Where I went:

What I did:

People I met:

Email addresses:

Phone numbers:

High point:

What I learnt about myself:

Budget:

	cash	credit card	debit card	travellers cheques
Accom				
Travel				
Food				
Drink				
Socialising				

Did you know?
In New Zealand there are approximately four sheep to every person?

diary

Where I went:

What I did:

People I met:

Email addresses:

Phone numbers:

High point:

What I learnt about myself:

Budget:

	cash	credit card	debit card	travellers cheques
Accom				
Travel				
Food				
Drink				
Socialising				

Quote:

"We always recommend that travellers don't look for (call centre) work in December or January. Do your travelling then, and come back to Sydney in February when the work begins to pick up again."

Kalena Jefferson
Sydney Operations Manager
Select Teleresources
Sydney

week 29: date -

diary

Where I went:

What I did:

People I met:

Email addresses:

Phone numbers:

High point:

What I learnt about myself:

Budget:

	cash	credit card	debit card	travellers cheques
Accom				
Travel				
Food				
Drink				
Socialising				

week 30: date -

Where I went:

What I did:

People I met:

Email addresses:

Phone numbers:

High point:

What I learnt about myself:

Budget:

	cash	credit card	debit card	travellers cheques
Accom				
Travel				
Food				
Drink				
Socialising				

week 31: date -

diary

Where I went:

What I did:

People I met:

Email addresses:

Phone numbers:

High point:

What I learnt about myself:

Budget:

	cash	credit card	debit card	travellers cheques
Accom				
Travel				
Food				
Drink				
Socialising				

☺ **Travel tip:**
"Open your mind to new cultures and traditions. It can transform your holiday experience and you'll earn some respect and be more readily welcomed by local people." From the Exploring The World Travellers Code produced by Tourism Concern.

 www.tourismconcern.org.uk

week 32: date -

Where I went:

What I did:

People I met:

Email addresses:

Phone numbers:

High point:

What I learnt about myself:

Budget:

	cash	credit card	debit card	travellers cheques
Accom				
Travel				
Food				
Drink				
Socialising				

diary

Where I went:

What I did:

People I met:

Email addresses:

Phone numbers:

High point:

What I learnt about myself:

Budget:

	cash	credit card	debit card	travellers cheques
Accom				
Travel				
Food				
Drink				
Socialising				

week 34: date -

Where I went:

What I did:

People I met:

Email addresses:

Phone numbers:

High point:

What I learnt about myself:

Budget:

	cash	credit card	debit card	travellers cheques
Accom				
Travel				
Food				
Drink				
Socialising				

☺ **Work tip:**
Use the wonder of email to contact agencies and employers before you arrive. Even if you can't sign up to agencies without an interview, it will show you are keen.

diary

Where I went:

What I did:

People I met:

Email addresses:

Phone numbers:

High point:

What I learnt about myself:

Budget:

	cash	credit card	debit card	travellers cheques
Accom				
Travel				
Food				
Drink				
Socialising				

Did you know?
New Zealand has no native mammals apart from bats and marine mammals such as seals? There are also no snakes in New Zealand.

www.doc.govt.nz

week 36: date -

Where I went:

What I did:

People I met:

Email addresses:

Phone numbers:

High point:

What I learnt about myself:

Budget:

	cash	credit card	debit card	travellers cheques
Accom				
Travel				
Food				
Drink				
Socialising				

diary

Where I went:

What I did:

People I met:

Email addresses:

Phone numbers:

High point:

What I learnt about myself:

Budget:

	cash	credit card	debit card	travellers cheques
Accom				
Travel				
Food				
Drink				
Socialising				

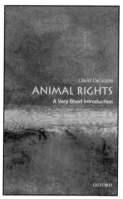
Quote:

"Most employers have no doubt that experiences gained from a well planned gap year involving projects, charitable work, a quality work placement or travel give students skills and added maturity which enables them to cope better with student life and seize future work opportunities."
Roger Opie, Director of Education
The Work Foundation

week 38: date -

diary

Where I went:

What I did:

People I met:

Email addresses:

Phone numbers:

High point:

What I learnt about myself:

Budget:

	cash	credit card	debit card	travellers cheques
Accom				
Travel				
Food				
Drink				
Socialising				

☺ **Work tip:**

It's been said before, but we'll say it again... the number one thing that agencies complain about travellers is their appearance, particularly in Sydney. Most temp agencies clients are corporate and expect temps to dress accordingly.

week 39: date -

Where I went:

What I did:

People I met:

Email addresses:

Phone numbers:

High point:

What I learnt about myself:

Budget:

	cash	credit card	debit card	travellers cheques
Accom				
Travel				
Food				
Drink				
Socialising				

week 40: date -

Where I went:

What I did:

People I met:

Email addresses:

Phone numbers:

High point:

What I learnt about myself:

Budget:

	cash	credit card	debit card	travellers cheques
Accom				
Travel				
Food				
Drink				
Socialising				

week 41: date -

Where I went:

What I did:

People I met:

Email addresses:

Phone numbers:

High point:

What I learnt about myself:

Budget:

	cash	credit card	debit card	travellers cheques
Accom				
Travel				
Food				
Drink				
Socialising				

☺ **Travel tip:**
When taking photos… "Don't treat people as part of the landscape, they may not want their picture taken. Put yourself in their shoes, ask first and respect their wishes." From the Exploring the World Travellers Code

 www.tourismconcern.org.uk

Where I went:

What I did:

People I met:

Email addresses:

Phone numbers:

High point:

What I learnt about myself:

Budget:

	cash	credit card	debit card	travellers cheques
Accom				
Travel				
Food				
Drink				
Socialising				

☺ **Work tip:**

Employers are looking for applicants who can prove that they are adaptable, confident, capable and good at working as part of a team and on their own initiative. Use your gap year experiences to show that you are all of these things.

week 43: date -

Where I went:

What I did:

People I met:

Email addresses:

Phone numbers:

High point:

What I learnt about myself:

Budget:

	cash	credit card	debit card	travellers cheques
Accom				
Travel				
Food				
Drink				
Socialising				

week 44: date -

Where I went:

What I did:

People I met:

Email addresses:

Phone numbers:

High point:

What I learnt about myself:

Budget:

	cash	credit card	debit card	travellers cheques
Accom				
Travel				
Food				
Drink				
Socialising				

✎   Remember...

There's no excuse not to stay in touch with loved ones while you are away. It has never been so easy or cheap to contact people long distance. Email is your most inexpensive option online, and you can use an instant messaging service like Microsoft Messenger to "chat" to people back home live online. You can also make discounted international phone calls. If you have a mobile phone, text messaging is cheaper than calling but be aware that you may be charged for receiving messages as well as sending them.

    http://messenger.msn.co.uk

week 45: date -

Where I went:

What I did:

People I met:

Email addresses:

Phone numbers:

High point:

What I learnt about myself:

Budget:

	cash	credit card	debit card	travellers cheques
Accom				
Travel				
Food				
Drink				
Socialising				

week 46: date -

Where I went:

What I did:

People I met:

Email addresses:

Phone numbers:

High point:

What I learnt about myself:

Budget:

	cash	credit card	debit card	travellers cheques
Accom				
Travel				
Food				
Drink				
Socialising				

week 47: date -

Where I went:

What I did:

People I met:

Email addresses:

Phone numbers:

High point:

What I learnt about myself:

Budget:

	cash	credit card	debit card	travellers cheques
Accom				
Travel				
Food				
Drink				
Socialising				

week 48: date -

Where I went:

What I did:

People I met:

Email addresses:

Phone numbers:

High point:

What I learnt about myself:

Budget:

	cash	credit card	debit card	travellers cheques
Accom				
Travel				
Food				
Drink				
Socialising				

Where I went:

What I did:

People I met:

Email addresses:

Phone numbers:

High point:

What I learnt about myself:

Budget:

	cash	credit card	debit card	travellers cheques
Accom				
Travel				
Food				
Drink				
Socialising				

✎ Remember...

Although Australia and New Zealand have similar laws and customs to western countries, other countries in Australasia do not. If you are travelling through Indonesia or Thailand for example, read up about local customs. If you are a woman travelling alone, avoid drawing unwanted attention to yourself by following local dress codes for women.

 www.fco.gov.uk/knowbeforeyougo

week 50: date -

diary

Where I went:

What I did:

People I met:

Email addresses:

Phone numbers:

High point:

What I learnt about myself:

Budget:

	cash	credit card	debit card	travellers cheques
Accom				
Travel				
Food				
Drink				
Socialising				

week 51: date -

Where I went:

What I did:

People I met:

Email addresses:

Phone numbers:

High point:

What I learnt about myself:

Budget:

	cash	credit card	debit card	travellers cheques
Accom				
Travel				
Food				
Drink				
Socialising				

week 52: date -

diary

Where I went:

What I did:

People I met:

Email addresses:

Phone numbers:

High point:

What I learnt about myself:

Budget:

	cash	credit card	debit card	travellers cheques
Accom				
Travel				
Food				
Drink				
Socialising				

personal details

Name:

Home address:

Home telephone:

E-mail:

NI number:

Passport number:

Tax File number:

Doctor telephone:

Blood group:

Dates to remember:

Flight dates & times:

my address book

AB

CD

EF

GH

IJ

KL

MN

OP

QR

ST

UV

WX

YZ

Name	Address/e-mail	Tel/mobile

my address book

Name	Address/e-mail	Tel/mobile

AB

CD

EF

GH

IJ

KL

MN

OP

QR

ST

UV

WX

YZ

my address book

Name	Address/e-mail	Tel/mobile

AB
CD
EF
GH
IJ
KL
MN
OP
QR
ST
UV
WX
YZ

my address book

Name	Address/e-mail	Tel/mobile

AB
CD
EF
GH
IJ
KL
MN
OP
QR
ST
UV
WX
YZ

my address book

Name	Address/e-mail	Tel/mobile

AB

CD

EF

GH

IJ

KL

MN

OP

QR

ST

UV

WX

YZ

my address book

Name	Address/e-mail	Tel/mobile

AB

CD

EF

GH

IJ

KL

MN

OP

QR

ST

UV

WX

YZ

my address book

AB	Name	Address/e-mail	Tel/mobile
CD			
EF			
GH			
IJ			
KL			
MN			
OP			
QR			
ST			
UV			
WX			
YZ			

my address book

Name	Address/e-mail	Tel/mobile

A

C

E

G

L

K

M

O

Q

S

UV

W

YZ

my address book

	Name	Address/e-mail	Tel/mobile
AB			
CD			
EF			
GH			
IJ			
KL			
MN			
OP			
QR			
ST			
UV			
WX			
YZ			

my address book

Name	Address/e-mail	Tel/mobile	
			AB
			CD
			EF
			GH
			IJ
			KL
			MN
			OP
			QR
			ST
			UV
			WX
			YZ

my address book

	Name	Address/e-mail	Tel/mobile
AB			
CD			
EF			
GH			
IJ			
KL			
MN			
OP			
QR			
ST			
UV			
WX			
YZ			

my address book

Name	Address/e-mail	Tel/mobile

AB

CD

EF

GH

IJ

KL

MN

OP

QR

ST

UV

WX

YZ

my address book

	Name	Address/e-mail	Tel/mobile
AB			
CD			
EF			
GH			
IJ			
KL			
MN			
OP			
QR			
ST			
UV			
WX			
YZ			